METAPHYSICS

METAPHYSICS

EMERICH CORETH *1919 -*

ENGLISH EDITION BY
JOSEPH DONCEEL

WITH A CRITIQUE BY
BERNARD J. F. LONERGAN

A Continuum Book
THE SEABURY PRESS • NEW YORK

First paperback edition 1973

THE SEABURY PRESS
815 Second Avenue, New York, N.Y. 10017

First published 1968 by Herder and Herder, New York
English translation copyright © 1968 by Herder and Herder, Inc.
This volume is an abridged edition of the original German edition, *Metaphysik,* copyright © 1961 by Verlagsanstalt Tyrolia Gesellschaft m.b.H., Innsbruck

Library of Congress Catalog Card Number: 68–21561
ISBN: 0–8164–2570–1
Printed in the United States of America

CONTENTS

CONTENTS

EDITOR'S PREFACE

SOME time ago, in *America* (September 24, 1966 and April 22, 1967) I made a plea for some continuity in the teaching of philosophy in our Catholic colleges. Although the "Letters to the Editor" were mostly unfavorable, I have not lost heart. The potshots came from both sides of the road, so that I have a feeling that I am on the right path. Some of my critics were dismayed because I was no longer satisfied with good, old-fashioned Thomism, the others were opposed to any systematic philosophy at all; they preferred the historical or the analytical approach. I have a feeling that among the people who do not write Letters to the Editor many were in agreement with me.

Evolution is generally better than revolution. That is why it seems preferable to keep part of the perennial philosophy, its substance, its soul. But, by all means, let us drop the obsolescent paraphernalia.

St. Thomas himself might be our best guide in this task. When inquiring whether our intellectual knowledge derives entirely from the senses (from the "phantasms," as he puts it), he answered:

Since the phantasms cannot of themselves immute the possible intellect, but require to be made actually intelligible by the agent intellect, it cannot be said that sensible knowledge is the total and perfect cause of intellectual knowledge; rather it is in a way the matter of the cause. (*Summa Theologica,* I, 84, 6, c)

We are told that sensible knowledge is *the matter of the cause* of our knowledge, that it is the *material* component of that which causes knowledge in us. What is the *formal* component of that which causes knowledge in us? What is the form of the cause of our knowledge?

In many passages of his works, St. Thomas explains that the form of the cause of our knowledge is metaphysics. Thus he writes:

As from the truth of the divine intellect proceed in the angelic intellect the inborn forms of things, according to which the angel knows everything, so from the truth of the divine intellect proceeds in an exemplary way into our intellect the truth of the first principles according to which we judge of everything. (*De Veritate,* I, 5, ad 5)

These "first principles" are the basic affirmations of metaphysics. St. Thomas tells us that they are virtually inborn in us.

As a being is, so it acts. Man is composed of soul and body. Therefore his activities too possess some kind of similar composition. One of the main human activities is the activity of knowing. It follows that human knowledge too must in some way, analogically, possess a soul and a body. The body of our knowledge is everyday and/or scientific knowledge. Its soul is metaphysics.

That is why metaphysics is *a priori,* virtually inborn in us, not derived from sense experience, exactly as the soul is ontologically prior to the body and not derived from it. Yet we would never know any metaphysics if we had no sense knowledge, exactly as our soul cannot operate without our body. Hence metaphysics is *virtually* inborn in us. We become aware of it only *in* and *through* sense knowledge, although it does not come *from* sense knowledge.

It follows that metaphysical truths are absolutely certain, in the sense that they cannot be denied without contradiction. If every one of our judgments is "animated" by metaphysics, a judgment by which we deny a metaphysical truth will be possible only because we affirm this same truth. We deny then explicitly what we affirm implicitly.

This is rather easy to show in many instances.

Thus, he who claims that nothing is certain contradicts himself, since he obviously considers this statement itself as certain. He who claims that all truth is historically conditioned implicitly makes an exception for his own statement and thus contradicts it. The philosopher who asserts that all philosophical systems are but rationalizations for repressed complexes thus invalidates his own assertion. When somebody tells us that only that which can be demonstrated scientifically is certain, we shall invite him to demonstrate his assertion scientifically. He cannot do it, since it is not a scientific but a philosophical assertion. He who claims that some things are totally beyond the reach of human knowledge speaks about these things and thus contradicts himself. When the bright young man states that it is wrong to hold any philosophical convictions, he admits implicitly that he is wrong, since this conviction he holds is itself a philosophical conviction.

Logical positivism died of such a contradiction. Its basic tenet was that a statement is meaningful if and only if it is either a tautology or empirically verifiable. But this statement is neither, hence he who affirms it admits in the same breath that it is meaningless. There are cases where the contradiction is less obvious. Thus, when a biologist denies all finality and design in evolution, because "ideas and purposes cannot influence physico-chemical processes," he contradicts himself. Uttering or writing this statement involves a great number of physico-chemical processes, the muscular contractions in his throat or in his hands, and these are obviously influenced by his idea and by his desire to express [a purpose]. (*America*, 116, 1967, p. 580)

These facts show that the affirmation of metaphysics is a condition of the possibility of every affirmation. But the philosophical method which investigates the conditions of the possibility of our knowledge has been known, ever since Kant's pioneering efforts, as the *transcendental method*. That is why the Thomism which we advocate might be called *transcendental Thomism*. The name may sound strange, since it combines the very new with the very old. But is there not much to be said for such a combination in philosophy?

If this conception of transcendental Thomism is correct, it follows that nobody can really "learn" it, since, previous to every learning, it is already at work in the learner's mind. He merely discovers what he has been holding unconsciously and affirming implicitly ever since the first stirring of his intellect.

Transcendental Thomism does not indoctrinate: it tries only to make the young mind aware of what it "always already" possesses. It uses Socrates' maieutic method: it is a nice example of intellectual midwifery, by which the student's mind is delivered of the metaphysical embryo it carried within itself. Turning the student loose too early and too freely into the labyrinthine mazes of philosophical history induces him to overlook his own intellectual activity, with its rich metaphysical content. It is slightly ludicrous to hear intelligent youngsters, who have "covered" all the great philosophers and are dazed by their contradictory claims, affirm with great conviction that "after all, nothing is certain, all our knowledge is historically conditioned," without being aware that they contradict themselves. They have probed the treasures of the great philosophical minds and overlooked the metaphysical wealth of their own minds. (*Ibid.*)

Among the metaphysical truths which man implicitly affirms in his every affirmation the most important is that of the existence of God. In a certain sense we cannot really "demonstrate" this truth, since we affirm it implicitly as soon as we set out to "demonstrate" it. In this sense, every "demonstration" of God's existence begs the question, since it takes implicitly for granted what it tries to demonstrate explicitly. That is why

10

transcendental Thomism prefers to speak of a "vindication" of our right to affirm God's existence.

He who wishes to "demonstrate" God's existence, starts from premises which are finite, contingent and relative, and hopes to arrive at a conclusion which is infinite, necessary and absolute. An impossible task. We cannot "arrive" at God; the distance is infinite. We start from him and we end up with him. He is present implicitly in the premises and explicitly in the conclusion. We reach God right away or never at all.

That we reach God right away can be shown by pointing to the fact that we know everything as finite and limited. But a limit can be known as limit only by him who is, in fact or in desire, beyond this limit. We are not beyond every limit in fact. But we are beyond every limit in desire, because we strive past it. Man is the being who is "always already beyond" every knowledge, every truth, every beauty, every possession and pleasure. Of every object which he knows man affirms that it *is*. He keeps striving towards an object about which he can really say that it *is*, that it fully exhausts the fullness of this predicate. Only the Infinite comes up to this fullness, only God really *is*. All other objects are *this* or *that*.

Such is the meaning of the *excessus* of St. Thomas, of the *dynamism* of Joseph Maréchal, of the *Vorgriff* of Karl Rahner and Emerich Coreth.

We can put it in another way by calling man the being which possesses an infinite horizon. The horizon which we see with our eyes is finite, we share it with the animals. The horizon which we know with our intellect is infinite. It is the horizon of being. This horizon of being is the main topic of the present work.

The main reason why transcendental Thomism has met so much resistance among American and British scholastic philosophers is the strong influence of Professor Etienne Gilson. This influence has, in general, been enlightening and invigorating, and American and British philosophy owes a debt of gratitude to Professor Gilson. Yet he refuses to use the transcendental method, because he is afraid that it might lead him into phenomenalism or idealism. That this is not necessarily the case has been brilliantly argued by Bernard Lonergan in his famous study "Metaphysics as Horizon." The author, the editor and the publisher are grateful to Fr. Lonergan for allowing them to reprint his paper as an appendix to the book. The reader himself will have to decide whether Fr. Lonergan is right when, at the end of his review, he prefers not to "equate metaphysics with the total and basic horizon." On this point the editor of the present English translation sides with Fr. Coreth against Fr. Lonergan, for it seems to him that "metaphysics, as about being," equates with absolutely every being, including the "subjective pole." The "incarnate inquirer" is a being, and nothing but a being. The fact that he stands in a social and historical context when verbalizing his metaphysical *a priori* is admitted by Fr. Coreth, who says so clearly and draws the necessary conclusions on pages 167–169. Fr. Lonergan claims that the method of metaphysics is only "one among many," which is quite true. He wishes it to be "considered from a total viewpoint." But is such a total viewpoint not the viewpoint of *being*? There is no viewpoint which is more total than this one. Hence the method of metaphysics must be considered by metaphysics. Metaphysics must justify its own method. That is what Fr. Coreth does explicitly in the second part of his Introduction.

Still, this minor difference of opinion does not detract from the basic agreement which exists between Fr. Coreth and the famous author of *Insight.*

The German title of this book is simply *Metaphysik,* and the subtitle describes it as *A Methodical and Systematic Introduction to This Discipline.* The author of the book, Emerich Coreth is Professor of Philosophy at the University of Innsbruck in Austria. The German original is a volume of 584 pages. There were good reasons for not translating the book in its entirety; instead, it has been condensed; an effort has been made to keep all its essential ideas, while omitting or abbreviating that which did not seem so important, especially some of the historical passages, which referred to German philosophy, and most of the references and the notes. The task was undertaken in collaboration with the author himself: he read every page of the condensed translation, he rewrote parts of his work for it, he suggested many changes and he approved the final draught. Yet no condensation ever comes up to the wealth of the original work, and it is to be hoped that many readers of this book, especially those professors who use it for their courses, will frequently refer to the original German text.

The author has kindly granted the translator great freedom in his enterprise. This proved especially useful in rendering such words as the ubiquitous and well-nigh untranslatable German word *Vollzug*. *Vollzug* is the noun derived from the verb *vollziehen*, which may mean: to perform, to accomplish, to fulfill, to act, to exercise, to actuate, to execute, to achieve and so on. Whenever possible, sentences containing the term *Vollzug* were reformulated, so that a straight translation of the word was no longer required. When this proved impossible, or too cumbersome, the word has been rendered by the English terms "actuation," "exercise" or "act." Fr. Lonergan uses "performance."

Another serious difficulty faced by the translator was the pair of words *Seiendes* and *Sein*. *Seiendes* means "that which is" and *Sein* is the being of that which is, it is that which makes beings into beings. In everyday usage both German terms are rendered into English by the same word "being." But this simple translation would never do in a book on metaphysics. Heidegger's famous "ontological difference" refers precisely to the important difference between *Seiendes* and *Sein*.

Several solutions were possible. The first one was to translate both terms literally, *Seiendes* as "being" and Sein as "to be."

That is what other languages do: *étant* and *être* in French, *ens* and *esse* in Latin. However, such a translation makes for clumsy English: metaphysics is abstruse enough in its own right and it seemed preferable not to burden it further with such unwieldly terminology.

Another solution was to translate *Seiendes* as *being* and *Sein* as *Being,* with a capital B. The trouble is that *Being* with a capital B makes the reader think, almost unavoidably, of the Infinite Being, of God. But throughout most of the chapters of the present book the word *Sein* does not directly refer to God, but only to the act of being, to that which makes beings into beings.

The solution adopted in this translation is very simple. Both *Seiendes* and *Sein* have been translated as *being.* However, when being stands in the plural or is accompanied by a modifier, an adjective other than *absolute* or *infinite,* it always stands for the German *Seiendes.* When it is used alone, or with the adjective "absolute" or "infinite," it is a rendering for the German word *Sein.* Thus *das Sein des Seienden* has been translated *the being of beings.* In the expression *material being* the word *being* renders the German *Seiendes. Seiendes als Seiendes, ens qua ens,* becomes *beings as beings.* Moreover, in quite a number of instances the term *Seiendes* has been translated by the unequivocal "the existent."

J. D.

METAPHYSICS

INTRODUCTION

1. THE HISTORY OF THE CONCEPT
OF METAPHYSICS

WHAT is metaphysics? We need to know the answer to this question, since it will help us determine the answer to many other questions, such as how metaphysics is possible, or how it can be validated and systematically constructed. It is impossible to answer these questions unless we know to some extent what is meant by metaphysics. We do not need a complete understanding of it, but at least some kind of nominal definition, some idea of what the tradition of philosophy means by this word. That is why we shall briefly examine at the very beginning the history of the concept of metaphysics.

(1) The first problem of Western philosophy in ancient Greece was the problem of the "origin of everything." Origin was meant not merely in the sense of what came first, but in the sense of what causes and maintains in existence, not only this or that reality, but all reality. This problem led Greek philosophy into the heart of metaphysics; for metaphysics is the science which investigates the ultimate ground of absolutely everything. The two aspects are essential: ultimate ground, absolutely everything. Metaphysics proposes a *final* answer to a *total* problem.

The distinction between what causes and what is caused is hinted at by the Eleatic philosophers and appears clearly in Plato. Beyond the concrete, individual, and changing objects of this world, Plato postulated an invisible realm of eternal, uni-

17

versal, and necessary essences. What can be perceived by the senses, said Plato, is only shadow and appearance (*mè on*), whereas the Ideas are endowed with real existence (*ontôs on*). The human mind is made for the world of Ideas, and transcends sense reality towards the suprasensible. Knowledge of the Ideas is the condition and the norm of our knowledge of the world. It is the task of philosophy to make this knowledge explicit, to show that the suprasensible is the only real reality. Thus philosophy is metaphysics, in that it is a science of the suprasensible, that is, of the universal and necessary Ideas, the causes and models of the visible world.

However, it was with Aristotle that the concept of metaphysics reached its full development. That part of his writings known as *Metaphysics* remains essential for any understanding of the nature of this science. Nevertheless, Aristotle himself did not use the term "metaphysics." It was Andronicus of Rhodes (first century B.C.) who gave to part of the master's work the name *ta meta ta physica,* or "what comes after the works on nature." Metaphysics treats of that which lies beyond the natural world of objects as their cause or ground. The title was so well chosen that it has been kept ever since for what Aristotle himself called *wisdom* (*sophia*) or *first philosophy.* It will be useful to investigate what Aristotle meant by these titles, so as to understand what metaphysics has meant for Western thinking from ancient time to the present.

Aristotle took the word "metaphysics" (or rather, "philosophy") in several different senses. A first meaning—first also in time, and deriving from Plato—was that metaphysics simply was the science of the suprasensible. However, since, unlike Plato, Aristotle derived the knowledge of the suprasensible from the knowledge of sense objects, he arrived at a second meaning of metaphysics, namely, that it is the science of the causes of all things, these causes being, for Aristotle, the material, the formal, the efficient and the final.

18

This second description leads to serious difficulties. In particular, the multiplicity of the causes endangers the unity of the First Science. This danger is obviated by a third conception of metaphysics, that it is the science of *beings as beings*.[1] Thus the object of metaphysics is all reality visible and invisible: whatever exists. It investigates all realities insofar as they are beings, it tries to discover what belongs to them in their quality of beings. Thus metaphysics, as the science of beings as beings, is the science also of the last causes of beings and the science of the suprasensible and divine being.

This third conception, however, produces a certain tension between two poles in metaphysics. On the one hand, metaphysics is described as the science of beings as beings, the universal science which investigates the totality of beings and all particular domains of beings. On the other hand, it is the science of the divine, of the primordial cause of all beings, it is (natural) theology.

Aristotle tried to solve the difficulty as follows. Theology, he said, studies the first universal cause of all reality. On the other hand, the science of beings as such must also investigate the first causes of beings, since it studies the totality of all that is. Thus Aristotle showed conclusively that theology, as the science of the divine being, and metaphysics, as the science of beings as beings, are intimately connected in their common effort to understand the ultimate causes of all reality.

(2) St. Thomas Aquinas adopted and developed Aristotle's position. In the Introduction to his *Commentary on Aristotle's Metaphysics* he distinguishes three aspects of this science, which correspond to three conceptions of the "first philosophy" of Aristotle. For Thomas, metaphysics is the science of God or theology, inasmuch as it considers God and the other suprasensi-

---

[1] As we said in the Preface, *on è on, ens qua ens*, is translated here not by *being as being*, but by *beings as beings*.

ble beings, the pure spirits. It is metaphysics insofar as it investigates beings and all that which belongs to beings as beings. And it is first philosophy insofar as it looks for the first causes of all things.

If the unity of a science demands the unity of its object, metaphysics, as conceived by St. Thomas, seems to lack such a unity because of its threefold object: beings as beings, the first principles of beings, and suprasensible beings, especially God as cause of all beings. Yet Aquinas defended the unity of metaphysics and vindicated it with even more emphasis than had Aristotle. He insisted that the immediate object of metaphysics is beings as beings. However, every science must investigate the causes of its object. In the case of beings as beings, these causes may be the extrinsic or intrinsic causes of each particular being: existence and essence, form and matter, efficient and final causes, as studied in first philosophy. Or the cause may be the universal cause of all beings, as studied in natural theology.

In its great lines this conception of metaphysics was held by all Scholastic philosophers.

(3) In the seventeenth century the concept of metaphysics was modified in various ways. First the stage was set for the ill-fated separation of the doctrine of God from the doctrine of being, in the system of Christian Wolff. Prior to him there had been the *Instauratio Magna Scientiarum* of Francis Bacon of Verulam, according to which philosophy is divided into three parts, treating respectively of God, of nature, and of man. These parts are preceded by and based upon a fundamental philosophical doctrine, *first philosophy,* which will later be called *ontology.* In this way, metaphysics, which as the combination of the doctrine of being and the doctrine of God was once the crown and conclusion of philosophy, now takes its place right after logic and before the philosophy of nature and the philosophy of man. As a result, it is turned into a formal discipline, a mere

doctrine of principles, which precedes the study of reality and loses all connection with the doctrine of God.

This development assumed its final form with Christian Wolff. In his classification of the philosophical sciences Wolff equated metaphysics with *theoretical philosophy,* thus considerably widening its object. He distinguished further between general metaphysics and special metaphysics. The former, also called ontology, is the basic philosophical discipline, which investigates beings as such. Hereby Wolff maintained the traditional conception of metaphysics. However, he held that the real task of metaphysics is to deduce, from clearly defined concepts and axioms, the statements which apply to every *possible* object of thought. In this way, metaphysics no longer is a real study of being, but a mere formal doctrine of axioms or principles. It is no longer rooted in being.

Wolff's special metaphysics is divided into three philosophical sciences, which he called cosmology, psychology, and (natural) theology. Thus he positively separated the science of beings from the science of God. Ontology, as the science of beings, no longer considers God, the first universal cause of beings. Consequently, either it turns into a formal and abstract doctrine of first concepts and principles, or, if it is to avoid this alternative, it has to adopt the makeshift solution of speaking of God as a mere hypothesis.

Wolff's classification, with all its inherent weaknesses, has been widely adopted by Scholastic philosophy, and only of late have resolute efforts been made to abolish it.

(4) Wolff not only modified the terminology and the classification, he totally transformed the very notion of metaphysics. He defined philosophy as the science of all possible things, insofar as they are possible. He was interested not in reality, but in mere possibility as such. For a rationalist like Wolff, possibility referred only to the possibility of thinking or conceiving

21

the objects without contradiction. The question that arises, then, is whether the object of metaphysics is still beings as beings, or whether it is the first principles of knowledge, from which may be deduced the rules that determine what mental contents are possible or contradictory.

Some of Wolff's followers held that the object of metaphysics is beings in general, or immaterial beings. Others considered metaphysics as the science of the first principles of our knowledge, from which derive the principles of all other sciences: metaphysics is no longer the science of beings, therefore, but the science of principles. To this latter group belonged Immanuel Kant's teacher, Martin Knutzen, and also Alexander Baumgarten, whose textbook Kant used for many years in his teaching of metaphysics. These facts help us, of course, to understand the development of Kant's thought.

According to these two thinkers, metaphysics studies not the real, but the possible. The doctrine of principles is totally separated from the doctrine of beings. Metaphysics has become a study of essences. Since the doctrine of principles had forfeited its foundation in being, the followers of Wolff were unable to discover an essential difference between metaphysical and other knowledge. The knowledge of the first principles differs from other, merely empirical knowledge, only in degree, not in kind, quantitatively and not qualitatively, insofar as it is the most universal kind of knowledge. In order to emphasize this essential difference, Christian Crusius, in the line of Leibniz, made the distinction between necessary and contingent truths. According to him, metaphysics considers only the necessary truths, that is, the truths which follow *a priori* from concepts. Thus metaphysics has ceased to be the science of beings as beings, it has become the science of the first principles of knowledge, insofar as they are universal and necessary.

(5) The foregoing allows us to understand Kant's position with respect to metaphysics. How is metaphysics possible as

a science? This question leads naturally to the question of the possibility of universal and necessary knowledge. In struggling with this problem, Kant proceeded beyond both rationalism and empiricism. Against rationalism, he maintained that universal and necessary principles cannot be merely analytic, that they must be synthetic, if they are to increase our knowledge; in other words, they must not merely explain what we know already, they must add something to our knowledge.

But synthetic judgments, Kant saw, which must be universally and necessarily true, cannot derive from sense experience, cannot be, in the sense of empiricism, synthetic judgments *a posteriori*. Sense experience refers only to the singular and to the contingent. Kant solved this problem by stating that there must exist judgments which are synthetic *a priori*, previous to experience, yet yielding really new knowledge. Thus the problem of the possibility of metaphysics becomes the problem of the possibility of judgments which are synthetic *a priori*.

This problem meets the question of the *a priori* in its full width and depth. Knowledge is to be understood from the previous conditions of its possibility. Thus we must turn our attention away from the object to our knowledge of it, or, as Kant put it, "to our way of knowing objects, insofar as this should be possible *a priori*." This is the *turn to the transcendental method,* which will determine the direction of the whole of post-Kantian philosophy. For Kant it meant a passage from the conditioned to the condition, from the object of experience to pure reason which determines this object. Thus metaphysics turns into transcendental philosophy. It is "pure knowledge of reason from mere concepts." "Hence metaphysics is a science of the basic concepts and principles of human reason," or, as we read in Kant's posthumous work, "Metaphysics is a logic of the pure intellect." "It comprises the *a priori* concepts and principles which bring together the multiplicity of empirical representations so as to make them into empirical knowledge, into experience."

23

Since reason must by itself determine its object, and since, on the other hand, it depends on the data of sense experience, it follows that, for Kant, the concepts and principles of pure reason are valid only within the domain of sense experience. Even within this domain they cannot determine the object as it is "in itself," but only as it appears to us. Such a metaphysics has no longer an objective, but only a subjective function; thinking is locked up in a mere "metaphysics of subjectivity." All this results from the fact that, long before Kant, metaphysics had lost its foundation in being. Kant's critique of pure reason is but the self-critique of a metaphysics without being, of a metaphysics of essence and of subjectivity.

Kant tried to save metaphysics by turning to practical reason, which, according to him, demanded as undeniable postulates the three basic realities which theoretical reason was unable to reach: the world, the soul, and God. Moreover, he endeavored to bridge the gap thus created between theoretical and practical reason in his *Critique of the Faculty of Judgment*. But his attempts were not quite successful.

Yet Kant's work was most significant in the history of metaphysics. First, negatively, it was the critical self-refutation of a metaphysics which no longer deserved the name "metaphysics." Kant has demonstrated once and for all that metaphysics is impossible without a return to being. At the same time, positively, he brought about the transcendental turn of philosophical thinking, which was to prove so important in modern philosophy. It is true that he took only the first step in this direction: he returned to finite subjectivity, thus cutting himself off from metaphysics. But his pioneering efforts must be continued, the self-actuation of the finite subject must be understood in the light of the conditions of its possibility, conditions which are previous to it and which transcend it. It must be understood in the light of being. Kant's critique forced metaphysics to think transcendentally and in a manner more critical and radical than his own, so as to overcome his critique through a return to the ultimate and unconditioned condition of all conditions, being itself.

(6) German idealism after Kant scorned metaphysics. It was equated with "dogmatic metaphysics," understood as an uncritical realism of the thing-in-itself, and contrasted with the transcendental philosophy of critical idealism. As an example of the latter, Johann Gottlieb Fichte introduced the *Wissenschaftslehre* (the theory of science) as a basic science whose content is the pure knowledge of reason, serving as the foundation of all other sciences, providing them with their basic principles.

In Fichte's system there is a new insight which overcomes the formal character of the first principles, as understood in rationalism and by Kant. This is that form presupposes content and derives from it, hence that a formal science, such as logic, presupposes a basic science, whose object is the primitive union of content and form. When, at the start of the *Wissenschaftslehre,* Fichte returned to the primordial certitude of the self-positing I, a new step had been ventured beyond Kant: the rediscovery of the real activity of the mind. Kant considered the pure "I think" only in its formal function, that is, as it contributed to determine the object of knowledge. Its own reality and actuality were overlooked. Not so with Fichte, who, instead of considering only the formal aspect, took into account not only the content of the mind, but also the very activity of the thinking Ego. This allowed him, in contrast to Kant, to reach all the way to an "I in itself" (*Ich an sich*). Although Fichte's early philosophy was subjective Idealism in its purest form, his thought soon proceeded beyond it, when he realized that thinking presupposes being: an absolute Being as condition of finite reason. In this way he drew near once more to the idea of metaphysics in the traditional sense.

This was even more the case with Friedrich von Schelling,

25

who advanced beyond Fichte. For him the Ego transcends itself and becomes aware of the Absolute, which lies before any duality of objective and subjective, of real and ideal, and enables us to "sublate" subjective into objective idealism. Although the way Schelling worked out his ideas in his philosophy of Identity was not devoid of difficulties, there can be no doubt that he intended, in fact, to build a metaphysics in the traditional sense of this term and that his thinking moved ever more clearly in this direction, especially in his later years. When he distinguished negative from positive philosophy, the "negative philosophy" stood for a pure *a priori* science of reason, whose validity is only relative. Schelling proceeded beyond it to a "positive philosophy" which, in the "ecstasy"—a necessary primordial affirmation of "being as previous to reason"—advances all the way to a doctrine of being, that comprises also a doctrine of God in which it has its foundation. Schelling has thus restored to metaphysics its former unity.

Schelling thereby went further than Georg Wilhelm Friedrich Hegel, in whose system the pure science of reason turns into an absolute science of reason. Hegel too, however, returned to the classic conception of metaphysics. Like Fichte and Schelling, he looked for an absolute starting point in philosophy, but unlike his two predecessors he did not discover it immediately in an intellectual intuition, but had to elaborate it by means of a transcendental study of conscious experience. In this way his *Phenomenology of the Spirit* brought him to "absolute knowledge," where logic turns into metaphysics. The transcendental-logical deduction takes into account not merely formal concepts and principles, as with the rationalists and Kant. As Fichte had already seen, formal elements are rooted in some content. There is no formal logic previous to some content of thinking. There is only an embodied logic, which determines the forms of thought through the agency of the contents of thought. The logic of Hegel was both an ontology and a theology, and in it we can

26

again recognize, although under a quite different form, the classic conception of metaphysics.

(7) With the decline of idealism in the nineteenth century, metaphysics began to be interpreted again in a manner quite different from the classic conception. Some opposed it to the objective sciences, as a subjective conception of reality. Others confined it to the domain of feeling, of practical faith, of irrational option. Still another group considered it an attempt to synthesize the data of the various sciences, the highest possible result of induction.

The beginning of the present century saw a number of thinkers return to the ontological problems, but quite a few of them did not go all the way to real metaphysics. Thus Edmund Husserl, who initiated the famous "return to the object," hence also the "return to ontology," spoke of "regional ontologies" (ontology as applied to the several domains of experience) which are topped by a "universal ontology" conceived, however, as a merely formal science. Nevertheless, on account of his phenomenological reduction, which forced him into a philosophy of mere essences, without connection with being, Husserl too locked himself in a transcendental idealism; he was unable to clear Kant's hurdles and reach reality. Husserl did not discover the road which leads to metaphysics or to metaphysical ontology.

(8) More interesting from our point of view is Martin Heidegger's idea of a *fundamental ontology.* Heidegger repeatedly insists that the whole of Western metaphysics has always considered beings, never being itself. It is interested in beings, not in the being of beings. Metaphysics, he says, is an *ontic,* not an *ontological,* way of thinking, because it pays no attention to the ontological difference between beings and being. It is a metaphysics of essences, which does not derive essence from being. Because metaphysics has forgotten being in behalf

27

of the beings, it is characterized by *Seinsvergessenheit,* or "oblivion of being."

Heidegger wants metaphysics to start with the problem of being. It must consider and firmly establish being, he contends, as that through which all beings are beings. But the question of being must first turn towards man, for more than all other beings, man, as *Dasein* (being-there), excells in the comprehension of being. When we meet or recognize beings, when we keep busy with beings, in any way whatever, this suppose that we stand before the horizon, against which beings as such manifest themselves to us; it supposes that we have some previous knowledge of that through which beings are beings: the being of beings. Man possesses a previous comprehension of being as the condition of his whole attitude towards beings. He is endowed with an ontological knowledge of being, through which he understands every being (*on*) through its ground (*logos*). "Man stands in the openness of being." Further, Heidegger endeavors to study this revelation of being in a systematic manner. Fundamental ontology thus becomes an "existential analysis of *Dasein.*" The whole of the existential constitution of man must be considered and reduced transcendentally to the *a priori* ground of its possibility, the being of *Dasein,* in which being as such reveals itself and makes possible our empirical or ontic meeting with beings and our activity about them. For Heidegger, fundamental ontology is essentially transcendental philosophy, which is concerned with the problem of the *a priori,* of the ontological *a priori;* in short, with being.

Heidegger uses Husserl's phenomenological method, yet he understands it in such a way that he cuts himself off from a real grasp of being. He does not consider human thinking as the place where being manifests itself. He hopes to find it in a more immediate and original way in man's pre-rational feelings and moods (*Befindlichkeiten*). But in this way he meets only with *human* being, being as man can experience it, finite and temporal being; he is unable to transcend it in a metaphysical understanding of being. For him, being is locked within the dimensions of finiteness and temporality, and this restriction prevents him from reaching real metaphysics.

(9) Yet Heidegger's basic problem deserves our attention. His summary judgment of Western philosophy may be unfair to some of the greatest thinkers within this tradition, he nevertheless points to real problems and tasks which the methodical reconstruction of metaphysics, on the basis of past experience, cannot afford to ignore. Since the time of Aristotle, classic metaphysics has considered as its object "beings as beings." This formula mentions only the beings, not the being of beings. But to consider beings as beings means to consider in them that which is common to all of them, which makes them into beings, namely, being. The fact that the classic definition mentions only the beings, not their being, as the object of metaphysics, intimates that being as such is never given to us as an object, that it reveals itself to us only in the beings whose ground it is.

No thinker of the past has been more clearly aware of the ontological difference than Thomas Aquinas, nobody has more clearly distinguished between beings (*ens*) and being (*esse*), or interpreted beings more consistently in the light of being.

It is true that his successors turned gradually more to a mere philosophy of essence, oblivious of being, unable to understand the beings in the light of being. This happened in later Scholasticism, and it happened with even more frequency in rationalism, in which the doctrine of beings as such turned into a doctrine of the first principles of thought, thus giving rise to Kant's critique.

(10) The purpose of these brief historical abstracts has been to show that the problem of fundamental ontology, the question

whether finite thinking is able to transcend itself and to reach the horizon of being as such, has always been a lively one in the history of metaphysics, that it has always arisen anew throughout this history, even if it has been given numerous conflicting answers.

Classically and traditionally, metaphysics is the science of beings as beings. It investigates beings in that which makes them into beings, their being. That is why metaphysics is the *basic* or fundamental science, since it investigates the basis, ground, or foundation of all reality. It is also the *universal* science, since it studies that which is common to all reality whatever. It can be the basic and universal science only because it pushes all the way to the ultimate unity or ground of everything, Absolute Being.

The *object* of metaphysics is never an object in the sense of a datum of sense experience; in order to know this object an act of thinking is required which penetrates into the data of experience and transcends them in the direction of the ultimate and the absolute, in the direction of being.

We have further learned from history that it is not even possible to establish the first foundations of metaphysics if human knowledge is not envisaged against the horizon of the Absolute. *A fortiori,* a complete system of metaphysics supposes a continual referring to Absolute Being, in whose light alone the being of beings stands revealed in its fullness and depth. We see, therefore, that both the history of metaphysics and the very nature of its problems show us that metaphysics is a bipolar science, a science of beings as such and a science of the absolute foundation of being.

History has provided us with a provisional notion of metaphysics, but the question remains whether and how what the tradition of Western thought understood and still understands by metaphysics is possible at all and how metaphysics as a science may be critically justified and constructed in the light of our modern awareness of its problems and methods.

2. THE METHOD IN METAPHYSICS

In order to determine whether metaphysics is possible as a science, we must establish what method it will have to use. A science is really a science only when it possesses its own method, and when it is aware of the nature of this method and capable of defending it.

(1) If this rule is binding on all science, it is especially binding on metaphysics, for, since it investigates an object which is beyond all sense experience, metaphysics cannot appeal to that experience in order to justify its own procedure. Other sciences may justify the methods they use by pointing to the results they reach. Metaphysics will never be able to use this pragmatic criterion.

The other sciences can also and do generally appeal to some higher science, when they wish to justify the method they use. No ordinary science can study its own method. Examining the method of physics is not a problem of physics, and investigating the nature of the historical method is not a historical problem. But how could metaphysics appeal to a higher science for the justification of its method, since it is the highest of all sciences?

Next, metaphysics cannot try out its method on its object, as other sciences do. In the other sciences, the object is first known in a pre-scientific way, and the method is tried out upon the object and slowly improved. As the object becomes better known, the scientist succeeds in ever greater degree in adapting his method to it.

All this is impossible in the case of metaphysics. Its object is beings as beings. But beings as beings are nowhere available ex-

31

cept in the mind of the metaphysician. We meet plenty of beings in our everyday experience, but never beings as beings. It is only by reflecting upon the beings of our experience that we can reach beings as beings. But this reflection is a metaphysical reflection. It uses the method of metaphysics. Thus there seems to be a vicious circle. We can discover the real method of metaphysics only by trying it out on its object; but we can discover the object only by using the method.

However, the problem itself contains the elements of a solution: would it be possible for us to inquire about the possibility of metaphysics if we did not from the very beginning know in some way what metaphysics aims at? Every question is made possible and is directed by some previous knowledge of the object of that question. When we inquire about a science which encompasses everything, that presupposes that we have already in some way encompassed everything. When we inquire about the possibility of a science of beings as beings, that presupposes that we know about beings as beings, that we know what makes a being a being, the very act of be-ing itself. Of course, this knowledge is not thematic or explicit. It is unthematic or implicit, presupposed by the very act of questioning, as a condition of its possibility. Hence we shall have to question the question itself, discover the conditions of its possibility. We must make the unthematic pre-knowledge into thematic knowledge. Hence the "object" of metaphysics, as it is from the very first contained in the metaphysical question itself, as a condition of its possibility, will determine the method of metaphysics. This method is called *the transcendental method*.

(2) Before developing this point, we wish to consider other methods which have been suggested for metaphysics. Since metaphysics is based not on direct observation but on reasoning, its method must imply reasoning. But there are two kinds of reasoning: the synthetic-inductive and the analytic-deductive kind. Both of them have been applied in metaphysics.

The synthetic-inductive method passes from the multiplicity of the concrete data of experience to the general laws which apply to absolutely all forms of experience. It tries to discover inductively what is true of every being as being. The unsound assumption behind this method is that the generalization of singular, contingent experiences can lead to the establishment of universal, necessary assertions. The inductive method leads to increasing probability, not to absolute necessary truth, and metaphysics is not satisfied with anything less.

Furthermore, other sciences are allowed to presuppose the validity of the process of induction; but metaphysics can presuppose nothing and should be able to justify the method of induction, something which can certainly not be done inductively.

Therefore, the synthetic-inductive method is unable to lead us into real metaphysical knowledge, and we seem to have no other choice than to use the analytic-deductive way. This method wishes, as its name implies, to derive the whole of metaphysics from a simple self-evident starting point, which it merely analyzes and from which it deduces all other metaphysical truths.

The presupposition, of course, is that the starting point pre-contains virtually the full extent of all our knowledge of beings as beings. But how can the truth of this presupposition be established beyond the possibility of any doubt, in an analytical or deductive way?

Moreover, even if this starting point were fully vindicated, we would then still have to use the laws of logic in order to derive all other verities from it. But we have no right to take the laws of logic for granted. Even these laws must be validated by metaphysics, and this again cannot be done by mere analysis and deduction.

(3) From all this it is evident that reasoning alone cannot be the method of metaphysics. For reasoning is *mediated* knowledge, it starts necessarily from some previous knowledge. Rea-

33

soning is done in syllogisms, which presuppose certain premises. Metaphysics, as the science which inquires about everything, will necessarily go back, from premise to premise, until it arrives at some knowledge or fact or experience which does not depend on any previous knowledge or premise, until it arrives at some undeniable, immediately self-evident truth.

But it must be well understood that metaphysics must avoid both essentialism and dogmatic empiricism. It would fall into essentialism if its starting point were a mere principle, a statement which is taken for granted because an examination of its terms shows that one term belongs necessarily with the other. For instance, the principle of identity, *Whatever is, is,* is undeniable, but by itself alone it does not lead us into reality. It means only that, *if* something is, it necessarily is. But it does not tell us *that* something is. We must start from some experience. Starting from a principle would confine us within the domain of possibility, of mere ideas or essences.

When we start from some experience, another danger threatens us, the danger of dogmatic empiricism. This consists in claiming to derive from mere sense experience something which is not really contained in it, which is affirmed without real justification, dogmatically. Here one claims to derive from a few particular experiences that which applies to all experience, from the observation of a few contingent facts that which is absolute and necessary.

We have seen how not to start metaphysics: not from mere reasoning, not from simple observation, neither through induction nor through abstraction. How then can we start to build the science of metaphysics?

It should be pointed out that, when we have a sense experience, we also have simultaneously the experience of having this experience; and this experience reaches much deeper than the sense experience. When we know an object (sense experience), we are also aware of knowing this object (intellectual intuition). In other words, every instance of sense experience contains elements which transcend that experience. The limits of sense experience can be transcended, because we always have already transcended them. Human knowledge can penetrate into the realm of metaphysics because it always occurs within that realm. Human thinking can reach being because it is always already with being. A critical justification of metaphysics is possible, because we can show that our thinking occurs essentially within the horizon of being. Some knowledge of being as such, of the basic determinations and principles of being, which apply to all beings as beings, is an *a priori* condition of the possibility of our every act of knowledge, even of everyday knowledge. A rejection of the possibility of metaphysics implies a contradiction between that denial and the act by means of which one denies, between the thematic content of the act and the unthematically co-affirmed and presupposed conditions of its possibility.

It is evident then that our starting point is not strictly *demonstrated;* it is, rather, *vindicated,* in this sense: that we can show that nobody can deny it without at the same time affirming it. We do really start from an immediate evidence, but this evidence itself cannot be demonstrated, except by showing that whoever rejects it, affirms it in his very act of rejection. In this sense, we have what Hegel called a *vermittelte Unmittelbarkeit,* a mediated immediacy.

(4) Such a way of reflecting upon the previous conditions of the possibility of an act of knowledge has been called by Kant the *transcendental method.* "I call every knowledge transcendental, which occupies itself not so much with objects, but rather with our way of knowing objects, insofar as this is to be possible *a priori.*" The aim of this method is to discover and to explain the knowledge which precedes and makes possible every knowledge of objects. This is not a knowledge which is explicitly

available before all other kinds of knowledge. It is rather a pre-knowledge, a basic knowledge, which enters implicitly into every kind of empirical knowledge, and which can be made explicit only through a reflection upon the previous conditions of the possibility of empirical knowledge.

This method was known long before Kant. Plato was aware that there exists a knowledge of basic principles in logic and metaphysics, which does not merely derive from sense experience, but which makes such experience possible. His doctrine of the Ideas is the first attempt made in Western philosophy to explain such *a priori* knowledge. St. Augustine professed a similar doctrine, when he attributed to a divine illumination the *eternal verities* present in the human mind. The Augustinian current within Scholastic philosophy remained faithful to this view. Thus St. Bonaventure explained our knowledge of the first principles through Augustinian illumination rather than through Aristotelian abstraction. St. Thomas too, who tried to combine the Aristotelian and the Augustinian traditions, was aware of the *a priori* conditions of human knowledge.

After him, however, the Aristotelian current grew so predominant within Scholastic philosophy, that this awareness became gradually dimmer and at last disappeared completely. It revived somewhat in René Descartes' conception of *inborn ideas,* although Descartes greatly exaggerated the clearness and distinction of human *a priori* cognition. We meet it again in the ontologism of Nicolas de Malebranche, albeit totally separated from experience and transformed into an intuition of eternal essences in God.

It was Kant who called this method *transcendental* and who really worked it out. But he did not go back far enough when looking for the conditions of possibility of human knowledge. He stopped at the finite subject, he did not reach an absolute horizon of validity, and thus he eliminated all possibility of metaphysical knowledge. Only if we can, against Kant and proceeding beyond him, show that our *a priori* knowledge is metaphysical knowledge of being, which opens for us the absolute horizon of being as such, shall we be able to validate metaphysics critically and methodically. This task has been clearly recognized within the neo-Scholastic school, especially since the pioneering work of Joseph Maréchal. But there remain a few basic problems which must be cleared up before we can begin to use the transcendental method.

The transcendental method uses a double movement, consisting of what we may call *reduction* and *deduction*. Transcendental *reduction* uncovers thematically in the immediate data of consciousness the conditions and presuppositions implied in them. It is a return from that which is thematically known to that which is unthematically co-known in the act of consciousness, to that which is pre-known as a condition of the act. Transcendental *deduction,* on the other hand, is the movement of the mind which, from this previous datum, uncovered reductively, deduces *a priori* the empirical act of consciousness, its nature, its possibility, and its necessity. Whereas reduction proceeds from a particular experience to the conditions of its possibility, deduction goes from these conditions to the *essential* structures of the same experience. The two movements are in constant interaction, they influence each other; yet it is possible to emphasize one over the other.

Thus Kant emphasized reduction, whereas Fichte and Schelling insisted more on deduction. In his *Wissenschaftslehre* Fichte started from an absolutely primordial datum, the absolute self-positing Ego. As it posits a non-Ego against itself, it determines and limits itself through this non-Ego. From this dialectic of the Ego and the non-Ego, Fichte then deduced the whole of experience. Something similar is found in the early Schelling, with this difference, that his starting point went even further back than the absolute Ego; he proceeded from the absolute point of indifference of subject and object, of Ego and non-Ego. These two

37

philosophers were able to do something which Kant felt unable to do, because they started from an undeniable "intellectual intuition."

Hegel disavowed this intuition and re-emphasized reduction in his *Phenomenology of the Spirit.* When he had reached "absolute knowledge," he used the deductive way, in his *The Science of Logic,* although in his own dialectical manner.

Husserl and Heidegger, too, emphasize the reductive way, as is to be expected in view of their phenomenological approach. While attempting to find out and to describe that which shows itself, they also look, each in his own way, beyond the phenomena, to that which is given together with them.

This historical background will aid us in devising the further course of our investigation.

(5) We have already seen how very important is the question of the *starting point* of any metaphysics. It must be absolutely first, presupposing nothing, from which all further knowledge can be derived; it must be solidly established and wholly undeniable. Hence our starting point cannot be a merely empirical datum, which is never undeniable and always presupposes other things, at least the subject to whom it is given. Rather, we should find out what conditions are required for the subject to have any knowledge at all, hence examine the conditions of the very act of knowledge.

But of what act of knowledge? If we take an act which has a definite content, do we not take for granted that this content is valid, that it can validly serve as a starting point for metaphysics?[1] Every starting point which we may consider can and should be challenged and questioned for its validity. This very fact suggests the answer to our inquiry. The correct starting

[1] Here is where we disagree with Maréchal, who takes the judgment as his starting point. A judgment has a definite content which cannot be taken for granted.

point is *the question itself*. The question itself cannot be challenged or questioned, it presupposes nothing, it takes nothing for granted. Should we nevertheless question it, then the question by which we challenge it will be the starting point. If we wonder about the very possibility of questioning, we will do so by questioning.

Furthermore, starting with the question itself is the only starting point which supplies us with a method for our inquiry. Every other starting point of a transcendental investigation takes two things for granted: the content and the method, that from which we start and the possibility of examining it transcendentally for its conditions of possibility. We need a starting point which does not take these two elements for granted but which establishes them. Only the question used as a starting point fulfills this condition. When we ask a question about the starting point, this question itself points to the question as the starting point. I must question the question. The verb of this statement shows the method which must be used (to question transcendentally the very act of questioning), while the object of the statement supplies the starting point (the question itself).

The central importance of the question in metaphysics derives from man's very nature. Man is the questioner, the inquirer, the wonderer, who discovers being more in the act of questioning than in any definite content of the mind, because being always extends beyond any knowledge, and man knows it as thus extending beyond anything he knows.

(6) Questioning the question would not make sense if there were not in the question more than what there seems to be at first. A question is an action and has a content. We pay attention to the content, not to the act of questioning itself. When we question the question, our attention is forced to proceed beyond the explicit knowledge presented by the content into the implicit knowledge contained in the act of questioning itself. Thus when

39

I ask what things I can question, the very act of asking this question supplies an answer to it. For I can ask questions about absolutely everything. Should somebody suggest that there might be limits to my power of questioning, I shall ask questions about these limits, and by this very fact proceed beyond them. The fact that I can question absolutely everything is unthematically contained in the very act of questioning. If I inquire what this "absolutely everything" about which I can ask questions really is, the answer to this question is likewise unthematically or implicitly contained in the question itself. For I always ask what everything IS. Hence I know that everything about which I can ask questions IS and that the range of my inquiring is the unlimited horizon of being.

We have here a continual interaction, a dialectic between concept and act, between *pensée pensée* and *pensée pensante*, between the conceptualized, explicit, thematic content of our knowledge and the unthematic, pre-reflexive, implicit knowledge that is co-affirmed with the act of knowing itself. This interaction results in what the German language calls *Vollzugswissen*, which might be translated as *knowledge implied in the act*, or more simply, *lived knowledge* or *exercised knowledge*.

The exercised knowledge is immediate, irrefutable, but unthematic. It must be made thematic through the mediation of reflection. When that happens, the exercised knowledge has been made thematic and answers the thematic questions.

But we must continue to ask questions. This constant asking shows that reflection has not exhausted the lived knowledge, has not yet adequately translated it into concepts. Reflex explicit knowledge is always surpassed by implicit exercised knowledge. Thus we penetrate ever more deeply into the mystery of human knowledge. In this dialectic between noema and noesis, between content and act, every new insight and every concept used to express it must be *mediated,* that is, it must be taken out of the immediate exercised knowledge through the medium of reflection. It is what Hegel called *mediated immediate knowledge, mediated immediacy.*

In this mediating reflection we find also a continual interaction between the two phases of reduction and deduction. When questioning the question, we go back to that which is presupposed by it and implicitly co-affirmed in it (reduction). Once we have discovered these elements, we can deduce from them the necessary essential structure of the act of questioning. There is a shuttling from fact to necessary conditions, from these conditions to the essential features of the fact.

(7) We come now to the problem of the relation between logic and metaphysics. Reduction and deduction are logical processes, occurring according to the laws of logic. Hence they seem to take for granted the validity of these laws. But in the study of metaphysics we may take nothing for granted, not even the laws of logic, much less their applicability in this very special domain, beyond the realm of sense experience. Logic cannot justify itself critically; such a justification is one of the tasks of metaphysics. Logically and ontologically, metaphysics comes before logic; chronologically, they originate together.

Hence we do not run into a vicious circle: in the self-justification of metaphysics, logic too finds its own self-justification, as the formal element implied in the act of thinking. Let us briefly show how this is so.

When, at the outset of metaphysics, we inquire about its starting point, we know already, as a condition of the possibility of such inquiring, what is meant by asking questions, we know about the difference between question and answer, about concepts which give a content to our questions, about the laws of identity and contradiction, without which the questions make no sense, about the relation existing between our thought and the language which expresses it, about the logical connections by which a certain question aims at a certain answer, and so on.

41

All this is unthematically co-known in the very act of questioning, otherwise we should be unable to ask meaningful questions. Hence here too it is possible, by applying the method of reduction, to make explicit the conditions of the possibility of the act of questioning—not its metaphysical, but its logical conditions. Since these are the conditions of the possibility of the act of questioning, and since we are in fact questioning, the questioning is possible and the conditions of its possibility are fulfilled.

Thus we see that logic is not presupposed by metaphysics, at least not as reflexive, conscious, scientific logic, and that logic as active, as exercised, is co-established and co-validated with metaphysics.

This reductive validation of logic should be followed by a deductive validation. If the laws of logic are conditions of the possibility of the act of thinking (reductively established), then it follows (deductively) that it is necessary for us to think according to such laws.

(8) We may now compare the transcendental method with a few other methods which have been used in metaphysics.

We use induction, since we start from experience. But this experience is not mere sense experience, it is an intellectual experience. And we do not, as is done in the other sciences, generalize from a few contingent instances, but we look for the *a priori* conditions of possibility.

We use deduction, but not in the manner of rationalism, which starts from inborn ideas or from some general abstract assertion. We start from unthematic pre-reflexive knowledge which must first be made explicit through the method of reduction and put into concepts. Hence we do not, like the rationalist, deduce from a mere idea, but from a real, existential self-actuation of the spirit, which manifests itself to us as endowed with a pre-reflexive metaphysical knowledge of being.

This is not idealism, for we hold that reality cannot be

deduced with logical necessity from a first principle, that it can be known only from experience.

This is not essentialism, for our deduction does not stay within the realm of mere possibility. Our metaphysics considers real being, the totality of all that which really is. It is in touch with reality because it starts from the reality of the self-actuation of our inquiring spirit, from which it proceeds to the rest of reality.

All in all, we stand nearer to idealism than to rationalism, to Hegel than to Wolff. We agree with the idealistic contention that we must start with the self-positing and self-mediating spirit, and that the spirit, even the finite spirit, manifests a real infinity in its self-actuation. But unlike the idealists we claim that the actual finiteness of the human spirit is not removed by its virtual infinity, that it can never grasp the Absolute in such a way that it can use it as the principle of an *a priori* deduction. The thinking of a finite spirit is not creation, but re-creation; it presupposes the infinite being, towards which it strives as towards the infinitely transcending horizon of all the knowable.

We use phenomenology to some extent, as we describe that which is given and try to uncover the pre-reflexive elements which are posited together with the act of knowing. But we differ from Husserl in two respects. First, we do not use his "eidetic reduction," which confines him to a consideration of mere essences, thus making of his philosophy an essentialistic philosophy. Secondly, we do not merely intend to describe that which is immediately given to a simple inspection of the contents of consciousness. For our metaphysical knowledge is not given to us thematically, it must be discovered by a transcendental investigation of the conditions of possibility of that which is immediately given in consciousness. Husserl himself moved gradually in this direction as he progressed in his phenomenological enterprise.

We might here use a distinction made by Heidegger between the popular meaning of phenomenon and its phenomenological

43

meaning. The latter refers to that which does not show itself at once, but must be made thematic, must be made to show itself. For Heidegger, however, even these deeply hidden contents are ultimately "seen" under more penetrating probing, whereas we claim that they reveal themselves only to reflection which uncovers what is implicitly co-affirmed in our knowledge. This is not to deny the fact that these contents are immediately evident, that they need no demonstration. Rather, our approach explains the nature of this immediate evidence, and in what sense we have here a case of "mediated immediacy."

Hence, in metaphysics, we never discover or demonstrate anything which is really new or unknown. Its only purpose is to explicitate the implicit, to bring out the animating principle of every kind of human knowledge. It makes abundantly clear that man is a metaphysical being and that his knowledge is metaphysical knowledge. Our method bases metaphysics as a science upon the self-actuation of the human spirit. It follows that this science possesses a plurality of aspects. It is transcendental-metaphysical *anthropology*, insofar as it investigates the *a priori* structure and laws of human self-actuation. Insofar as it discovers in this way the being of all that which is, it is transcendental-metaphysical *ontology*. Finally, insofar as it shows that spiritual self-actuation and the knowledge of being implied in it are intelligible only against the background of the Absolute, it is transcendental-metaphysical *theology*. Yet these three aspects constitute an indivisible unity; none of them can be investigated without taking into account the two others.

As for the method of metaphysics, it discovers and validates itself in the very investigation. This is true of all sciences, it is true also and especially for metaphysics. We have briefly explained its nature in this Introduction. Throughout the following development, methodological considerations will accompany the direct study of the main topic.

I.

THE QUESTION AND BEING

AT the beginning of metaphysics comes the question about its starting point. This question cannot be avoided. The starting point determines the further development and contains the whole system in germ. If we select the correct starting point, we shall be able to bring our task to completion. That is why the correctness of the starting point can be fully shown only at the end. Here, however, the question about the starting point can only be a question about that which comes undeniably first, which presupposes nothing else, which validates itself in its possibility and its necessity, thus providing a firm basis for further reflection. Hence our first task is to discover the starting point and to derive from it the method for all further inquiry. Now, the starting point is the question about the starting point, which turns into the question about the question, thus leading into further inquiry. This inquiry shows us that the condition of the question is being. For every question is a question about being, which we always already know, yet must always further inquire about, without ever being able to grasp it in fully comprehensive knowledge.

1. THE QUESTION

The Question as Starting Point

(1) At the beginning of metaphysics comes the question about its starting point. The starting point must be that which comes first, before which there is nothing else, from which we may begin. The question about the starting point answers itself by inquiring at the beginning about the starting point. The starting point is the question about the starting point. This question is unquestionable and presupposes nothing. Should it be questioned or should we try to find out whether it presupposes something, we arrive at another question, which posits once more the possibility and the necessity of the question. So we must and can ask the question about the starting point. This question comes first, it cannot itself be further questioned, and it needs no further justification of its possibility or necessity.

The question is the most critically radical starting point which may be conceived. In whatever way we intend to start off our reflections, we must at least ask questions. Giving up all questioning means giving up all thinking. Whatever starting point we may wish to choose, we cannot avoid the question about the starting point. Every other starting point may and must be questioned, for we must inquire whether they are fitting ones. Prior to any starting point comes the question about it. The question alone is the first, self-justifying, unquestionable starting point.

(2) All the other starting points which have been suggested can be questioned about their validity. Hence they all ultimately lead to the question: Is this one the right starting point?

Thus a certain number of neo-Scholastic philosophers start with the *judgment* (Maréchal, Lotz, Marc). This method resembles ours, insofar as these authors try to establish meta-physics by demonstrating that the absolute affirmation of being is a condition of the possibility of every judgment. However, if they use a particular judgment, it has a content, whose validity we may question. If they use judgment in general, the absolute position implied in every judgment, then we may inquire about the right they have to make such absolute judgments. Practically, however, the difference between this method and ours is not very great.

If, with St. Augustine and Descartes, someone wishes to start from methodical doubt, doubting everything which he can doubt, until he arrives at an assertion which can no longer be doubted, we should inquire whether he can doubt everything, whether he has a right to do so, whether methodical doubt is really the best method. And we are back at the question.

Others have suggested the dialogue as the starting point (Brunner), and have pointed out that the question itself is a form of dialogue. Hence we should inquire whether the dialogue is the correct starting point; and thus we are back again at the question as our starting point. Although the question takes its origin in dialogue, it goes deeper than the latter, since it can call the dialogue itself in question.

Contemporary philosophers like to take their starting point somewhere in the history of philosophy, and this is justifiable since human thinking is essentially historical and needs the stimulation of the history of thought. He who wishes to study metaphysics must first inquire into what the historical tradition understands by metaphysics, and how it has methodically tried to develop this science. But these are questions again. Furthermore, we must also inquire whether the history of metaphysics is really the best starting point and can provide us with the right method for building a metaphysics.

That is why we prefer to start with the question. It is quite true that every possible reality or statement can be investigated for the metaphysical conditions of its possibility, since everything IS. In this sense, absolutely everything may be used as a starting point.

But all these starting points suppose that we take them for granted, they do not validate themselves; whereas the question about the starting point is, as we have seen, self-validating, and provides us with the method to be used in metaphysical inquiry.

The Question about the Question

(1) We start our metaphysics with the question about its starting point. We have seen that the question itself is the starting point. Thus the question about the starting point has become the question about the question. We question the question. Our question may be poorly expressed, it may be absurd, unanswerable; but when we question it, we again ask a question and thereby affirm the possibility of questioning. Nobody can, without implicit contradiction, question the possibility of questioning.

Thus it is not the *content*, but the *act* of questioning [*der Vollzug*] which is undeniable. Every content may be called into doubt, may be questioned. But the act of questioning itself cannot be called into doubt, for it is confirmed by the question which calls it into doubt. This act is conscious, aware of itself, otherwise we could not reflect upon it. Every question contains a nonthematic, implicit awareness of the act of questioning. The question about the question must investigate this awareness of the act of questioning, and find out what is implicitly affirmed in it.

(2) We shall, therefore, use a dialectical method, which resembles that of Blondel more than that of Hegel, although it differs from both. Our dialectic is not, like that of Hegel, a dialectic of concept and concept, but, like that of Blondel, a

dialectic of concept and act, of that which is thought and the act of thinking it.

Hegel's dialectic develops within the domain of concepts. A first posited concept produces out of itself and opposes to itself a second concept. Between the two of them there arises a contradiction, which is "sublated" [aufgehoben] in a third concept, the dialectical unity-in-contradiction of the two first concepts. Thus the first concept is enriched, deepened, and determined by the second concept.

Blondel's dialectic is different. The concept derives from a reflection upon the living action. But the first concept which is thus posited is insufficient, it is transcended by the fullness of action. Hence there is the need to oppose a second concept to the first one; between the two of them there is an opposition, not a contradiction. Yet their unity would be unintelligible if it were not discovered in the action itself. But when this unity is put into concepts, it is once more seen that action is richer and fuller than this mere unity; and thus the dialectical movement continues.

We too discover a dialectic between concept and act, between a thematic knowledge which can be expressed in concepts and a pre-conceptual, unexpressed knowledge, co-posited unthematically in the act. This knowledge is immediate, and undeniable, but it has to be translated into concepts. Yet conceptual thematic knowledge can never exhaust the implicit exercised knowledge, it is always exceeded by the richness of the act. We try to derive everything from a starting point which establishes and justifies itself transcendentally: the act of questioning. In this process we must "mediate" [vermitteln] not only every new insight, but also every new concept which will be used, that is, we must discover it in the very act of questioning and in its implications. Hence the main difference between our procedure and that of Hegel and of Blondel is that we start with the question, which validates itself and provides us with the method to be used in our investigation.

The Question about the Conditions of the Question

(1) It is impossible to deny the possibility of asking questions. Thus the question about the question does not deny or question the possibility of asking the question, but it inquires about the conditions of this possibility. The question about the question has turned into the question about the conditions of the possibility of asking questions.

(2) But there seems to be a difficulty. We chose the question as starting point, because it presupposes nothing, because it is unconditioned, and now we speak of the conditions of the possibility of the question.

In order to resolve this difficulty a distinction must be made between the ontic conditions and the logical conditions of an act. An *ontic* condition is one whose *existence* is presupposed by the act, but which does not itself enter into the act as one of its constitutive elements and is not co-affirmed in the act. Hence it cannot be derived or deduced from the act. We are not interested in such conditions at present.

A *logical* condition is one whose *knowledge* is presupposed by the act, which enters into the conscious act and is implicitly co-affirmed in it. It is not a condition of the possibility of the act, but of the validity of its content. Thus when a false judgment is affirmed, the act of affirmation is possible, but the affirmation is false, because its logical conditions are not fulfilled.

Every question has logical conditions, since some kind of knowledge, albeit unthematic, is presupposed and co-affirmed in it. A question, insofar as it is this or that question, not insofar as it is simply a question, may be invalidly asked, but it is nonetheless possible to ask it. Hence insofar as the question contains some content, it has logical conditions, which are the conditions of the validity of the co-affirmed content; they are not the conditions of the very act of questioning. For a question as question posits nothing, as such it has no logical conditions. We can always ask questions, as this act justifies itself. Hence we can also, without any logical conditions, question the question, inquire further about the question. Insofar as the question as such excludes all logical conditions, it is simply unconditioned and without any presuppositions.

Therefore, when we inquire about the conditions of the question, it can only be about the conditions of the possibility of the *act* of questioning, about conditions which are unthematically co-affirmed in the very act of questioning. We call such conditions *transcendental* conditions. They resemble the ontic conditions, because they are conditions of the possibility of the act, not simply of the validity of its content, as with logical conditions. They resemble the logical conditions, because they enter into the very act, they are co-affirmed in it, they are not simply presupposed, as with ontic conditions.

Hence the transcendental conditions are, strictly speaking, conditions of the possibility of the act, they are co-affirmed, although not thematically, in the act itself. It follows that the fulfillment of such conditions is demonstrated by the act itself. Transcendental conditions are not properly presupposed, but co-affirmed. Ontic or logical conditions are presupposed, either as actually fulfilled or as known, while transcendental conditions are conditions of the possibility of the act, unthematically co-affirmed in the act.

This answer resolves the problem of whether the question is conditioned or unconditioned, mediate or immediate. It is both, depending on the point of view. The question is unconditioned insofar as it has no logical conditions. But it depends on transcendental conditions, whose fulfillment is guaranteed by the question itself, because the conditions are co-affirmed in the act of asking the question. The question about the question is, therefore, a question about the transcendental conditions of its possibility. We may call it the transcendental question about the question.

(3) Kant too was interested in this transcendental question, but again his was an approach which differs considerably from ours. Kant inquired about the conditions of the possibility of the phenomenal object, as it appears in the mind. These conditions will come to light only insofar as they are co-affirmed with the phenomenal object as its *formal* determinations. In other words, Kant considered only the *content* of knowledge, not the *act* of knowledge. His approach was static, not dynamic. As a result, he shut himself up in the phenomenal order, he was unable to reach the domain of metaphysics.

Hegel's attitude was ambivalent. On the one hand, he tried to grasp thinking in its real actuality and to put it at the basis of his system. But as he believed that he could adequately translate the act, the actuality of thinking, into concepts, he lost the act, he mistook the concepts for the act, he ended up in a merely conceptual dialectic. He did not get beyond a formal philosophy of essences, which was unable to reach the full reality of being.

Husserl too considered only the content, not the act, and he professed essentialism. Heidegger uses the transcendental method in order to discover the conditions of possibility of human self-actuation. He tries to find what makes it possible for man to understand *Seiendes* (that which is). But because he considers only the act, not its content, because he overlooks the essence in his quest for real being, because he does not want to translate what he discovers into conceptual language, he gets lost in phenomenology and does not really penetrate into metaphysics.

From all this it is clear that we are confronted with a continual dialectic of *act* and *content,* both of which must be considered and investigated. The act and that which is unthematically co-affirmed in it must be expressed in concepts, transformed into content. Yet this conceptual thinking, the content, must never lose touch with the act, which always transcends it, which can never be exhaustively expressed in it. The concept must stay rooted in the act, explicit knowledge must feed on the knowledge implied in the act, on what we have called *exercised or lived knowledge.*

The Pre-Knowledge as Condition of the Question

(1) Every question presupposes certain things. We can question only when we do not yet know that which the question is about, otherwise there is no need for a question. On the other hand, we can ask questions only if we know something already about the object of the inquiry. Otherwise, we do not know what question to ask. Hence the possibility of the question contains two elements which the German language expresses as *Fraglichkeit* and *Fragbarkeit.* Both mean: the possibility for a question to be asked. *Fraglichkeit* means the possibility of asking the question because we do not know the answer as yet. *Fragbarkeit* means the possibility of asking the question because we know enough to ask a pertinent question. In other words, the possibility of the question implies that it *should* be asked (*Fraglichkeit*) and that it *can* be asked (*Fragbarkeit*). The former aspect refers to my not-knowing, the latter to my knowing something about the object of the inquiry.

Hence questioning is possible if there is within us a mixture of knowing and not-knowing. In order to be able to ask the question we must know something, not everything, about the topic in question.

This is not a simple juxtaposition of knowing and not-knowing, a knowledge surrounded by ignorance. Such a combination does not yet constitute a question. It is rather a knowing not-knowing, a knowing ignorance, aware of its own ignorance, hence proceeding beyond the limits of its own knowledge, and anticipating, in some kind of pre-knowledge, that which it does not know as yet. Such a knowing ignorance begets the desire to know and evokes the question. We may call it the *pre-knowledge of the question.*

(2) This pre-knowledge is never given explicitly in the question. Explicit are the not-knowing and the desire for knowledge. It is given implicitly. Otherwise, the question as question would be impossible.

It is to be understood that, in the question, the pre-knowledge is not questioned, but remains presupposed. It is true that the question emphasizes not that we know, but that we do not know, that we wish to know; but the question is made possible by the pre-knowledge which, in the very act of asking the question, is unthematically co-affirmed, and is no longer questioned.

Furthermore, this pre-knowledge is not only unthematic, it is also unfinished, undetermined, it refers to further possible inquiry. It is a knowledge which transcends itself into non-knowledge. But it is no longer put in question itself; despite its incomplete character, it is the solid framework within which the question is made possible. This pre-knowledge of the question might also be called its *horizon,* since it is the background against which the question stands out.

2. THE PRE-KNOWLEDGE OF THE QUESTION

The Pre-Knowledge of the Single Question

But what single question shall we thus examine? Can we take any question at random? Random questions may have logical presuppositions. If they are not validated, we are not sure that we have a right to ask these questions. Hence only one question may be considered: one whose right to be asked has been established, the initial question about the correct starting point of metaphysics. For we have shown that this question is self-justifying and self-validating.

Yet this question presupposes a considerable amount of knowledge. We must know what metaphysics is, at least in general. We must know what a starting point is. All that we know about metaphysics and its possible starting points constitutes the background of our question and influences its meaning and its direction.

(1) Yet all this does not enter into the question in the same way. Much of it is not co-affirmed in the very act of asking the question. What we know, what we have heard, read, or thought about metaphysics and its starting point, is previous to our inquiry, it does not enter into it as co-affirmed. It is not strictly a condition of the possibility of the act of questioning. We could ask the same question without this or that bit of knowledge. Hence a transcendental analysis cannot reductively discover all this information in the question. Yet this knowledge influences the question and modifies its meaning for me. The same question means something at least slightly different for different people, because of their different backgrounds. If in general we call *co-knowledge* knowledge that precedes the question and enters into it in some way, we may call the knowledge of which we are speaking here *the modifying co-knowledge* of some specific question. It is not a condition of the possibility nor a constitutive element of the question, it merely modifies the meaning of the question for the questioner.

(2) Other elements enter more deeply into the act of questioning, in such a way that they are conditions of the possibility of this particular question and are thus co-affirmed in this act

of questioning. When we inquire about the starting point of metaphysics, we must know what metaphysics is or wishes to be, what a starting point is, that metaphysics has a starting point. This kind of knowledge is a condition of the possibility of this question, it can be derived from it reductively. We call this knowledge *constitutive co-knowledge,* because it is co-known, although unthematically, in the question. It is co-affirmed as known. This co-knowledge is a condition of the possibility of the question, insofar as it is this particular question, not insofar as it is simply a question.

(3) Hence this co-knowledge is not a constitutive element of the question as question, it does not explain the movement of the question beyond what is known, into the unknown. When we inquire about the starting point, we inquire beyond our present knowledge of possible starting points into something which we do not know as yet: the correct starting point.

In general, whenever we ask the question *What is this?,* we must already know about *this,* our knowledge of *this* is posited as co-knowledge in the question. But we know also that it points to a further *what,* which is not known yet, and which *this* is. We inquire about it, because we do not know it as yet, *and* because we know it already as something as yet unknown. This anticipation [*Vorgriff*] of the as yet unknown constitutes the question as question, makes the question possible, not as this question, but simply as a question.

Here we do not simply have certain contents which are present as conceptual anticipations of some of the features of the object under inquiry. Such contents derive from the constitutive and from the modifying co-knowledge. These two kinds of knowledge anticipate something of the content of the object, they do not constitute the movement of inquiring anticipation itself. This belongs only to something which goes really beyond what is already known and gropes towards the unknown. It is a pure pre-knowledge, a pure transcending of what is already known, a pure anticipation of what is not known yet. We call it *pure* because it does not derive from any empirical content of the question, nor does it contain any content of that kind. For such contents do not explain why the mind strives past them towards something else. This pure pre-knowledge, as the movement of pure surpassing and pure anticipation, is *the constitutive condition of the possibility of any question whatsoever.*

(4) We have shown how this kind of pure pre-knowledge is present in our question about the right starting point of metaphysics. We can also show how it is present in other questions. Thus when we ask, *What kind of book is this?* we must know what a book is, that this object is a book (co-knowledge). This knowledge stands in the wider context of our knowledge about books in general, about books of a certain kind, a context which modifies for us the meaning of the question. But inasmuch as the question aims at what we do not yet know, it gropes beyond all this information. This groping is animated by our pure pre-knowledge, which makes the question possible as a question.

If we express the same ideas in Husserl's terminology of the horizon, we may put it as follows: The single concrete question is conditioned by constitutive co-knowledge and is accompanied by modifying co-knowledge. Hence it stands in a context of previous knowledge, it has a background of previous information, which constitutes its horizon as a single question. This is a limited, partial horizon of possible questions, an empirical horizon constituted by the questioner's own past experience. Every single question possesses such an empirical horizon. These partial empirical horizons presuppose, however, a previous encompassing total horizon of all questioning and of all knowledge, which is no longer empirical, but purely *a priori.* We shall

57

try to show that the question as question presupposes, as a condition of its possibility, such *a purely a priori total horizon,* and that this total horizon is the horizon of *being.*

The Pure Pre-Knowledge of the Question as Such

(1) From all this it is already evident that only the pure pre-knowledge can really help us in our metaphysical enterprise. The modifying co-knowledge, obviously, cannot, since it is not a condition of the possibility of the question; hence we cannot derive it from the question by reduction. It is true that the constitutive co-knowledge is a condition of possibility and can be derived reductively from the question. But this co-knowledge is not self-validating; it has logical presuppositions of its validity which have not yet been made explicit and which cannot yet be made explicit. Moreover, co-knowledge may be false. The question, not as question, but as this particular question, may be senseless, unanswerable.

(2) Hence it would seem advisable to eliminate the co-knowledge. But is this possible? Every question is a single question, determined by some definite co-knowledge. Since this co-knowledge is always questionable, it seems that every particular question remains questionable.

But if every question is questionable, we are naturally induced to inquire about it, to ask the question about the question. We should try to find whether this question can be asked, whether it is a legitimate question. And thus a new question arises, which once more establishes, by its very existence, the possibility of asking questions.

This new question is no longer conditioned and determined by the co-knowledge of the former one. It has, of course, some co-knowledge, which makes it this particular question. But this

58

co-knowledge is nothing but our knowledge of the fact that we asked the former question. Hence this co-knowledge is not something random, something which has not yet been made explicit. The co-knowledge of the questionable question has now been eliminated, or rather transferred into our knowledge of asking that question. The question has become the question about the question. It has become self-aware, aware of itself as a question. We may, of course, again question this new question, insofar as it is this particular question, and thus question its co-knowledge. Once more, however, this co-knowledge is transferred into our awareness of asking the question which we are now questioning. And so we can go on and see that it is possible to eliminate the co-knowledge by transferring (*sublating*) it into the awareness of the act of asking the following question. Co-knowledge can be eliminated in the question about the question.

(3) All of this shows that the possibility of asking questions in general, questions as such, does not depend on the possibility of asking this or that question. The contrary is true: we can ask individual questions because we have the power of asking questions in general, because we possess the power of questioning.

This power of questioning in general is not conditioned by any co-knowledge, otherwise we should never be able to eliminate the latter. This power is conditioned only by the *pure pre-knowledge,* which belongs to the question as question. It is this pure pre-knowledge that we must now examine.

(4) We have already said a few things about the combination of knowing and not-knowing present in every question. While knowing this determined content, we know that we do not know everything about it, that our knowledge is limited. But to know a limit as limit is already to be beyond this limit. Hence we know that there is more to know, we anticipate

59

further and deeper knowledge. We must now investigate this pure anticipation of the questionable as such.

The Pure Anticipation of the Questionable

This pure anticipation is a movement which gropes forward, in a certain direction. But in what general direction does this groping proceed? Three answers are possible:

(1) The ultimate aim of this groping is always something well determined, known as such, at least in its main outline. This anticipation is possible because it is based on some previous well-determined knowledge, which directs the anticipation. Hence the pure pre-knowledge would simply be a projection from our knowledge of previous objects unto other possible objects.

All of this applies to the co-knowledge, which is a condition of possibility of every single question. It does not apply to the pure pre-knowledge, which is a condition of the possibility of the question as such.

(2) The anticipation proceeds towards some totally undetermined knowledge, towards the absence of every determination.

It is true that it goes beyond every concrete and singular determination, deriving from any particular knowledge implied in any single object. But this absence of determination is not a total absence of determination. A movement towards nothing is not a movement. A question which aims at the totally undetermined would not be a question. Hence we have a relative indetermination, a relative nothing, which does not exclude every positive aspect.

(3) Therefore, the ultimate aim of our groping is neither totally determined, nor totally undetermined. It possesses a positive aspect. Where shall we discover this positive aspect? In the

pure pre-knowledge of the question as such, of the act of questioning in general.

We may inquire only about that which may be inquired about. And we may inquire about everything which may be inquired about. Hence the ultimate aim of the question as such is the questionable as such, insofar as it is questionable, the totality of the questionable, the pure horizon of the questionable.

Of course, the possibility of every single question is conditioned by a determined aspect of that which is questionable. But we can question the possibility of such a single question. Hence we can continue to inquire beyond every single determined aspect of the questionable. The question, as such, is not made possible by any determined aspect of the questionable. If, then, the question as such must be made possible by some pre-knowledge of the questionable, it can be made possible only by a pre-knowledge of the questionable as such, by a pure anticipation of the questionable as such.

The Pure Anticipation of Being as Such

(1) It is easy to show that the questionable as such has no limits. For if there were limits, we would ask questions about them, and, by so doing, we would pass beyond them, do away with them. Hence the questionable as such is simply everything, the horizon of the questionable as such is unlimited.

It is only because, in final analysis, man is always inquiring about everything, that he can inquire about particular things. The limited horizon of every single question is always comprised within the unlimited horizon of the question as such.

(2) Man always inquires about everything, not, of course, about every thing in particular. Such kind of questioning would never reach an end. Hence the question about everything must

be a question about everything at once. And this implies that everything must constitute a unity, the unity of all that we may inquire about, the unity of all the questionable. This unity is a condition of the possibility of the question as such.

(3) This unity is the unity of *being*. For, whenever we inquire, we inquire about the being of things. What IS this, that, everything? Hence being as such is the ultimate aim, the unlimited horizon of every question. This totality of being is not the sum of all previously known beings, but the anticipation of the totality and of the unity of all beings, present to the human mind as the unthematic pre-knowledge of every question.

Hence we have demonstrated that the possibility of inquiring about being as such and in its totality is the condition of the possibility of every single question.

The Pure Anticipation of Being in its Totality

(1) To inquire about being as such is to inquire about all beings inasmuch as they are beings. It is, therefore, to inquire about that which makes them all exist as beings, their *esse,* their act of being. The ultimate aim of our questioning is thus the act of being.

(2) Hence the anticipatory knowledge of the act of being is the condition of the possibility of every question. We are, to some extent, aware of this fact in our everyday experience. When we inquire: What is this, why is this, what for, where, when is this so?, we inquire about particular determinations of beings. But all of this presupposes that the thing about which we inquire IS, and pre-knowledge of this act of being is co-affirmed in our question. The same applies to existential questions: IS there such a thing? IS there really something which

possesses the act of being? Even when we do not have the answer to that question, even when we are simply inquiring, we must know, if our question is to make sense, what is meant by this "act of being."

We may inquire whether there IS anything at all, whether the act of being, which causes things to be, is a reality, is something. But all of this presupposes pre-knowledge of this "to be" and of its meaning. Moreover, these questions get their answer in the very *act* of questioning. When we inquire whether anything really is, we are aware that our act of inquiring and that we, the inquirer, really *are*. This awareness is implied in our awareness of the act of inquiring, in our lived or exercised knowledge. Here again the explicit question is answered by the implicit lived knowledge.

(3) Hence we have squarely landed into metaphysics. Every question ultimately aims at being as such, at that which causes beings to be, at the act of being.

We have already remarked that the being whose pre-knowledge is a condition of the possibility of the question, is not the sum total of all beings. It is not reached by induction, but rather by anticipation. It is not a totality resulting from previous partial knowledge, but the previous total framework in which every partial knowledge fits. It is the horizon within which every particular act of knowledge occurs. It follows also that this totality of being is not, at least not explicitly, being as the first cause of all reality. That the act of being is the innermost principle of every single existent will have to be shown subsequently.

Since every question turns ultimately into a question about being in its totality, which is thus the condition of the possibility of the question as such, it follows that we know about being in its totality and that we do not know everything about it. We know about it, otherwise we could not inquire about it.

63

We do not know everything about it, we want to know more about it, otherwise there would be no need and no sense inquiring about it. This shows that man is congenitally a metaphysical being, who cannot help inquiring—at least implicitly—about the totality of being, since he cannot go through life without asking questions.

3. BEING AS THE HORIZON OF THE QUESTION

Being as the Unconditioned

(1) When we ask questions, we do not only want to know how things are in relation to us, in a phenomenal way. We want to know how they are absolutely, in themselves. In other words, we do not only want to know how these things are imagined or thought by us or by human beings, perhaps necessarily, because of the way we are made. We do not only want to know about them within a restricted horizon of validity. As long as we receive only this kind of answer, we continue to ask questions about that which IS, as it really IS.

We want to know not how or what being is FOR US or FOR somebody or something, but what it is IN ITSELF, absolutely, for every being capable of knowing the truth. Hence only unconditioned, absolute being can put an end to our questioning.

(2) It might be objected that we only want to know what things are for us. But it is not difficult to show that this objection is refuted by the very act of questioning. Even if explicitly we inquire only about a relative validity for us personally, this relative validity itself is posited as absolute. It is absolutely so that things appear to us in such or such a way. Thus behind the relative horizon there is always an absolute horizon.

Moreover, we would not even be able to inquire about an unconditioned validity, if our question were basically locked up within the scope of conditioned and limited validity. But we can inquire about absolute validity. We can speak of "validity for me" only because we contrast it with "validity in itself." There is a contradiction latent in all forms of idealism and of relativism, in their claim that our knowledge is valid only for us, not in itself. They make a distinction between that which is valid for us and that which is valid in itself, and they imply that this difference is valid in itself, not merely for us. In other words, merely subjective validity is limited validity. But he who is aware of a limit as such, is already beyond that limit. The relativist can assert the limited validity of human knowledge only by transcending it. He affirms that it is absolutely valid to say that human knowledge is only relatively valid, and thus he contradicts himself.

(3) Hence the horizon of our questioning is the unconditioned. It is the unconditioned which is expressed in the word IS. Because and inasmuch as it is, that which we inquire about is unconditioned. Hence being appears as the unconditioned, the absolute; it is the unconditioned condition of all questioning, it is the absolutely necessary.

Being as act exists in itself, as a totality, as the ultimate and unconditioned, within whose horizon we can inquire about single realities or about all reality. This is always and necessarily presupposed as the condition of every question and is co-affirmed in the very act of questioning. Otherwise, we should not even be able to ask a question.

(4) What we have said does not include a demonstration of God's existence. When we showed that the act of being (esse) is unconditioned and ultimate, we meant only the act of being in general. We did not explicitly mean an Absolute Being as

ultimate foundation and cause, existing beyond all finite beings.[1] From this absolute nature of being in general we can derive the existence of God only by differentiating and distinguishing it from finite and conditioned being. Hence we do not begin by presupposing finite beings which are conditioned and contingent and argue from the conditioned to the unconditioned, from the contingent to the necessary. For it is impossible to know the conditioned or the contingent as such, except against the horizon of the unconditioned and of the necessary. We start by establishing the unconditioned and absolute nature of being as a whole, which is presupposed and co-affirmed in every question, as a condition of its possibility. Later we shall show that the questioner himself, since he can never reach being as a whole, since he is always striving towards that aim, grasps himself as finite being in a context of finite beings, thus setting himself off from the unconditioned being. Only then will it be possible to know the finite as a conditioned being, and this knowledge presupposes, as its unconditioned condition, the existence of an Absolute Being.

Being as the Unlimited

We have shown that the act of being posits itself as unconditioned. This unconditionedness implies that the act of being cannot be transcended, that there is no going beyond it, that it is unlimited, infinite.

(1) If the horizon of our knowing were limited, our knowledge would not be absolute. We could then occupy other points of view, with other horizons, where things might look different to us. Within a limited horizon we would not even be able to ask about the ultimate, absolute, unconditioned point of view.

---

[1] That is why in the following pages we shall speak of *absolute being,* not of *the* Absolute Being.

This question itself transcends every finite horizon. Hence, in order to penetrate into the *intensively* deepest core of being, we must also reach the *extensively* widest range of being. That which constitutes the ultimate, unconditioned reality of things is *being,* and that which affects absolutely everything, without any limitation, is likewise *being.* Being is therefore the ultimate reality, both intensively and extensively. And the horizon of being, within which we ask the question as question, is simply unlimited.

(2) The unlimitedness of the horizon of being is negatively confirmed by Kant, who restricted human knowledge both extensively and intensively: extensively, to the object of sense experience; intensively, to their phenomenal aspect. Kant was right in combining both restrictions. A knowledge which is restricted to *some* objects only of reality cannot know these objects in their *full* reality.

On the other hand, he who knows things in an absolute, unconditioned way, can also know absolutely everything; the horizon of his knowledge is unrestricted, without any limits.

(3) We can now see, therefore, how the transcendental method differs from the critical method. A critique of knowledge starts from a single content, whereas the transcendental method makes sure at once of the total horizon, within which knowledge occurs. What are the advantages of the latter approach? If we take a single content as starting point, even the most undeniable, such as *I am,* it remains always possible that this certitude is valid only within a limited domain. Kant's objection is difficult to refute: this knowledge is a phenomenon, something which is true "for me," we do not know whether it is true in itself. It is a fact that, in every case of true knowledge, the total horizon of absolute validity is co-affirmed, as a condition of the possibility of this knowledge. But this co-affirmation

should be made explicit, if we want a critical justification of our starting point. Therefore, the transcendental method is more critical than the ordinary critique of knowledge. It goes beyond the single affirmation (however undeniable this affirmation may be) and it investigates the conditions of its possibility.

One might object that the total horizon can be discovered only through an analysis of single phenomena. Only if we are sure of the validity of our single acts of knowledge may we conclude to the validity of this horizon. This objection carries only if we start with the judgment, not when we start with the question, as we have shown above. The question presupposes nothing, at least no determined content. Where it does, it is possible to eliminate this content and arrive at the pure question, which leads us directly to the total unconditioned horizon of being.

II.

THE QUESTION
AS ACTUATION OF BEING

1. BEING AND KNOWING

WE have shown that the condition of all inquiring or questioning is the horizon of being, as unconditioned and illimited. But with the universal and empty horizon of being we do not know as yet what kind of beings are to be found in the totality of being. The pure knowledge of being does not give us any specific knowledge about being, it does not tell us what is and how it is. However, our starting point was not pure being, but the question. The act of questioning already presupposes a difference: the difference between knowing and not-knowing. We can ask questions only if our knowledge anticipates some answer; yet we can ask questions only if our knowledge is still incomplete. It is a condition of the possibility of questioning that we should know about being and also that we should not know about it. We must examine the act of questioning from this double point of view.

(1) Questioning or inquiring presupposes some *knowledge about being*. But this knowledge, through which we "anticipate" in the direction of being as a whole, is not a grasping possessive knowledge, but an anticipating projecting knowledge; it is not a knowledge which possesses that which is known, but a knowl-

69

edge which projects that which can be known. This presupposes that we already know about being or about the meaning of being. The origin of this knowledge lies in the act of questioning itself. Whenever we question, we know that we question, that we are the inquirer, that we perform the act of inquiring. In every act of inquiring or knowing, some being is given which coincides immediately with knowing, which knows itself as being. The act knows itself as being. Being knows itself as act. We have an immediate *unity of being and knowing in the very act of knowing.*

This immediate identity is the origin of every knowledge about being, since no other being is as immediately given to us as the self-knowing act of inquiring or knowing. Here we discover on the one hand the original *meaning of being:* as being in itself, as simple being-posited. This being is not yet given as an object, but as the being of our own self-knowing act. The meaning of being as an object is a secondary, derived meaning. On the other hand, we also discover the *meaning of knowing.* Knowing is not something different from and extrinsic to being; it is merely the self-possession, the self-luminosity, the self-presence of being in the original identity of being and knowing. Knowing about something else, about an object, in the opposition of subject and object, is a derivative, not the original sense of knowing.

(2) The question presupposes that we know about being. But it also presupposes that *we do not know about being.* Otherwise, we would be unable to question. Therefore, since our knowledge about being consists in the identity of being and knowing, our not-knowing about being consists in the non-identity of being and knowing. To being as known is opposed being as not or as not yet known. When we question, we know about the *difference* between being and our knowledge, about the *transcendence* of being with respect to our knowledge. We know

that being exceeds us and our knowledge; otherwise, we would be unable to inquire about it.

Yet this difference or non-identity is posited in the unity of being. For I, the inquirer, *am;* and the other, the object of the inquiry, *is.* Being encompasses both in the same way. Likewise, the difference or non-identity is posited in the unity of knowing, insofar as it is a knowing about being. When we inquire we know not only about the being of our act, we know also—by anticipation—about the being of that which we do not know, about which we inquire. This not-knowing too is comprised within knowing. We know that we do not know, that we do not know everything. In our knowing not-knowing we proceed beyond our limited knowing towards that which we do not know. But we proceed beyond it in and through knowing; only this proceeding beyond makes inquiry possible.

2. SUBJECT AND OBJECT

When we inquire, we know ourself as the inquirer and we know about something else which stands over against us as the object of our inquiry. When we know, we know ourself as the knower and something else as that which is known. The duality of inquirer and that about which he inquires, of knower and that which he knows, is that of *subject and object.* Insofar as, in the one act of inquiring or of knowing, we know of both of them, ourself and the other, both—subject and object—are posited in the same act. In the identity of the act we posit the difference of subject and object. This is true not of the subject and the object *in themselves,* but of the subject and object *in the act* of knowing, that is, of the subject and the object insofar as in the unity of the self-knowing act they are posited and opposed to each other. But the difference of subject and object *in the act* presupposes the difference of the subject and the object *in themselves.*

(1) Whenever we inquire about something, we must already know about it, otherwise we would be unable to inquire about it; to this extent the object is posited in our act of inquiring. When we inquire about it, on the other hand, we do not yet know it entirely, in everything that it is, otherwise we would no longer be able to inquire about it; to this extent it is not posited in our act, but presupposed by it. We do not inquire— and we can no longer inquire—about that which we know already, that is, about the object as contained in our act of knowing. But we inquire—and we can only inquire—about that which we do not know as yet, that is, about the object inasmuch as it is not yet posited in our act of knowing, inasmuch as it exceeds this act and is presupposed by it. Hence it is a condition of the possibility of the question that it should proceed beyond the object as posited in the act, in the direction of the *object in itself.* The latter is necessarily presupposed, as something that *is* in itself, that is not yet fully known, that should provide an answer to the question and a content to our knowledge.

(2) Even as the object contained in the act of inquiring presupposes the object in itself, the subject as acting presupposes the *subject in itself.* When we inquire about something, we know ourself as the one who inquires and wishes to know. We know ourself as the selfsame subject of the present inquiring and of the possible future knowing. We can inquire only because we know of the possibility of knowing. Hence in the act of inquiring we are presupposed as a subject, who is more than the subject in the act of inquiring, who is also the subject of this future act of knowing. The subject as acting presupposes the *subject in itself.* Should this not be the case, we would be unable to inquire, since we would be unable to look out for some

knowledge which, as the selfsame subject, we anticipate already as our future knowledge, as the answer to our question.

This shows that the difference of subject and object in the act of inquiring, a difference which is posited in the identity of this act, is conditioned by the difference of subject and object in themselves, which is necessarily presupposed in the act of inquiring.

3. FORMAL AND MATERIAL OBJECT

We have discovered in the act of questioning a difference in identity, consisting in the opposition between the subject and the object of the activity of knowing: they are identified by this activity, yet they are rooted in a subject in itself and an object in itself, that are really distinct or opposed to each other. This opposition itself is comprised within a higher unity, within *the identity of being.* For we know about ourself, the inquirer, as really *being;* and we know about the object of our inquiry as something which *is.* Being encompasses both of them: the being which is identical with ourself and that which is not, the being posited in our act of knowing and that which exceeds this act. Hence not only the subject and the object of our act of knowing, but also the subject and the object in themselves, are encompassed by this identity.

(1) This identity is an identity in difference, that is, an identity which does not do away with the difference, which really comprises non-identical realities. It is a case of unity in multiplicity, of unity in diversity, which occurs only when that through which one differs from the other is distinct from that through which one agrees with the other. Such a determination, which belongs to a being without wholly coinciding with it, is called a *form.* Hence the identity in difference is *a formal iden-*

73

tity, the common possession of an identical form. It is opposed to the real identity by which a being perfectly coincides with itself.

We know about the formal identity of being in the real difference of beings—subject and object—in and through our act of knowing. The same act makes us aware of the difference between being and our own activity, since we inquire about beings which are other than ourself. Hence in and through our act of inquiring or knowing we know about our own being and about being as such, which is more than our being and which encompasses every reality. We may call this difference the *ontological difference,* the difference between a being which we are ourself and being as the being of all beings, which transcends us. This difference, which is always already posited in our every act of knowledge, is the condition of the possibility of our inquiring about other things, and of our knowing about them.

(2) When we inquire what this is, we must already know about *this,* which is given to us as an object; but we do not yet know its *what,* about which we inquire. We know it already as something which *is* in the formal identity of being; and we know it as something different from us, facing us as the object of our inquiry, in the real difference existing between beings. Thus we discover a duality in the object: that through which it *is,* and through which it agrees in formal identity with all that which is; on the other hand, that through which it is this or that particular thing, really different from all others. Hence beings do not disappear in the formal identity of being, they remain distinct from other things. Thus we notice that the possibility of inquiring or questioning presupposes as one of its conditions a duality which traditional philosophy calls the duality of the *material object* and the *formal object.* For we can inquire only if we know already, about the object of our inquiry, that it stands in the formal identity of being. On the other hand, our

inquiring presupposes that we do not know everything about the same object, that it possesses other features which are not yet given together with the formal identity of being.

(3) We must now determine in general the nature of and the relation between material and formal object; this will help us explain the idea of horizon. Next we must find out, by examining the act of inquiring, what its formal and material object are; this will allow us to explain in what sense being as formal object is the horizon of all inquiring and of all knowing.

We call that about which we inquire or that which we know the object of the inquiry or of the knowledge. The *material object* is the object as it presents itself in its unity and totality, as object in itself. On the other hand, the *formal object* is a certain aspect or point of view under which it appears when we inquire about it or know it in a certain manner. In this way, the various sciences differ from each other not only through their material object, but also, especially when several of them study the same material object, through their formal object. But the formal object is not only a formal determination in the object, which makes it appear to us from this or that point of view; it is also a peculiar angle from which we must inquire or know about the object so that we may see it from this point of view. In the former case we have *the formal object as object,* that is, a formal determination, belonging to the object and which becomes itself the object of such specific inquiring or knowing. In the latter case we have *the formal object in the subject,* a formal determination which belongs to the act of inquiring or of knowing itself, previously to all knowledge.

This distinction allows us to explain the notion of horizon. The horizon is the material object, as the totality of all possible single objects, insofar as *a priori* it is projected and determined by the formal object in the subject; it is the range of objects which are determined by the formal object as object.

We have seen that every question supposes, as a condition of its possibility, a previous knowledge about being; hence it presupposes the *horizon of being,* outside of which a question about that which *is,* is impossible. We can inquire about this or that being only if we can inquire about beings as such; if we can inquire about beings as such, we can inquire about every being. It follows that *the material object of the intellect is every being.* This is possible only because the formal point of view from which we question beings is not a particular or restricted one, but simply their being, by which they *are* and through which they agree with everything else. Hence the formal object of our inquiring is being as being. *The formal object of the intellect is being as being.* Since the formal object does not single out a particular aspect of the beings, but coincides with the material object, with beings as a whole, the possibility of inquiring extends to whatever *is* and reaches it in everything that it is. Inquiry or the question extends as far as being.

The horizon of the question derives from a pre-knowledge that is never thematic itself, but which conditions and determines every thematic question. We have seen that this pre-knowledge of being is based upon our exercised or lived knowledge, through which we become aware of the unity of being and knowing. This exercised or lived knowledge never becomes thematic; likewise, our pre-knowledge of being is never thematically given. Never do we know merely about being as being, without knowing at the same time about some being or at least without inquiring about some being. Being is never given as an object. But the pre-knowledge of being conditions and determines every inquiry about beings, it projects the horizon of being as the horizon of all possible inquiry.

Being is never given as object, but only as the formal object in the subject. The formal object as object is not being, but beings, although we can inquire and know about them as such only in the light of our pre-knowledge of being.

76

III.

BEING, ESSENCE AND ACTIVITY

INQUIRING or questioning is an activity of being, but not of being itself and as a whole. It brings about the identity of being and knowing, but also the distinction between being and knowing, since the inquirer knows and knows not, differentiates himself from the object of his inquiry, hence also from being as it surpasses him. The act of inquiring is an activity of being, but of the being of a finite something, of a finite essence. Hence inquiring supposes a finite being, which is composed of the act of being and essence. But the activity of inquiring is more than the being composed of the act of being and essence; it is the performance of an activity which proceeds beyond the finite being. Thus we discover, as one more condition of inquiring, the possibility and the necessity of activity. Hence in this chapter we shall examine being in relation to *essence* and in relation to *activity*.

1. BEING AND ESSENCE

The Finiteness of the Existent

(1) The question reveals the ontological difference between beings and being: beings are, they are posited in and by being, but they are not being itself and as a whole. This difference

77

implies the finiteness of beings, of the inquirer and of the object of his inquiry.

When he inquires, the inquirer knows about being as it surpasses him, he knows about the transcendence of being with respect to his own being. He knows that he is limited, that he is a *finite being,* that is, something which is, but which is not being itself. It follows that not only the finiteness of the inquirer, but also his awareness of it, is a condition of the possibility of the question. It is not, or not necessarily, a thematically explicit knowledge, but an unthematic knowledge, implied in the activity of inquiring itself.

(2) The inquirer generally does not inquire about being as a whole. As a rule he asks: What is this or what is that? He wishes to know the peculiar features of single people or things, posited as beings, as finite beings. The finiteness of the object of our inquiry is a condition of the possibility of questions referring to single beings. Should the object of our inquiry not be finite, single questions would be impossible, and we should be able to inquire only about being as such.

(3) It follows that the question manifests the *finiteness* both of the single inquirer and of the single thing which is the object of the inquiry. But finiteness means limitation in being: beings are, they possess being, but they do not possess it in fullness; on account of their limitation they are distinct from other beings and from being as a whole. This finiteness of the beings is a condition of the possibility of all inquiry. Every inquiry supposes some not-knowing, thus revealing the finiteness of the inquirer. Every question reveals a not-knowing of the determining, limiting features of some thing, thus revealing the finiteness of this thing. We must now investigate the ontological foundation of this finiteness.

Being as the Principle of Reality

(1) About every thing we may ask two basic questions: *whether* it is and *what* it is. The first question inquires about the thing's *act of being* (*is-ness, that-ness, existence*); the second about the thing's *essence* (*whatness*). Should something possess no act of being, but only an essence, it is a mere possible, not something real. The real differs from the possible because to its essence is added its act of being. Both of these determinations, which our mind distinguishes in the thing, are really present in it. Both concepts represent realities. Otherwise, the thing would not be real (act of being) or it would not be this or that (essence). Moreover, these two determinations are distinct from each other, at least in our mind.

It follows that the act of being is that in the existent which makes it real, which distinguishes it from a merely possible thing, which posits it as really existing. The act of being is the inner principle or ground of that which really is; it is the inner ground through which beings *are* in themselves.

(2) But about every being we may also inquire *what* it is. It possesses a *whatness,* a certain amount or degree or content of being. This whatness itself is real, is something which is. Since the act of being is that through which every reality is real, the whatness of each existent receives its reality from the act of being of the same reality.

Thus we cannot conceive of the act of being, of existence, simply as a mere state into which a previously constituted essence would somehow be transferred. The act of being is rather that which makes real whatever is real, including all determinations of the existent, including its whatness. Being is the v   [1] ground or principle of all existents and of their determ

(3) Should it be objected that every being possesses *its own* well-determined being, that the unity of being is only the product of an abstraction, we would reply that this conception leads not only to nominalism but to an absolute pluralism. The whole of reality would disintegrate, fall apart, without any common feature, into an unrestricted plurality and diversity. We would be unable to have a common concept of being. Such a concept presupposes in its object some community in diversity, some unity in multiplicity. The concept of beings as such presupposes that all of them share being. Hence it follows that being is the principle of all real determinations of all beings.

(4) But how can being be the principle of determination? For determination implies limitation, and being knows no limits. For a limit is necessarily a limit separating from something else. A limit which does not separate from anything is not really a limit. Hence that from which the limit separates must be something positive, it must be, or at least it must be possible. But whether it really be or be only possible, in both cases it is posited in its reality or in its possibility by being. Hence, since everything from which being could be separated by a limit can only be being (real or possible), being cannot be separated from anything by a limit, being by itself knows no limit. Hence it can only be the principle of unlimited determinations, of an unlimited content of reality.

Therefore, if finite beings possess real determinations and a limited content of reality, this situation cannot derive from being itself, but requires a principle distinct from being, which imposes the limit. In the concrete fullness of its determinations every finite being is posited by being; it is posited within its limits by some other principle. Hence there exists a principle of limitation, of determination, which is distinct from being, the principle of the positive content of these determinations. It is called the *essence,* and we shall examine it in the following pages. But first let us append a brief historical note.

(5) For centuries, Thomists and Suarezians have been arguing the topic of the *real distinction* between existence and essence, between the act of being and essence. Both agree that every finite being is composed of two constitutive elements, which the Thomists call *esse* (the act of being) and *essence,* and the Suarezians *existence* and *quiddity* (whatness). They disagree when the former claim that between these two components there exists a real distinction, that one is not the other *in the things* which they constitute through their union, whereas the Suarezians maintain that, in the things themselves, there is no distinction between both components, that the distinction exists only *in our mind.*

Lately the discussion has lost much of its actuality, and we shall say only a few words about it. The important point in the Suarezian position is that it does not admit being as an inner principle previous to every being. It does not go beyond each existent towards its previous ground, it does not inquire about its ontological constitution. It is an *ontic,* not an *ontological,* way of thinking. When about some existent we ask whether it is and what it is, the Suarezians claim that this question does not inquire about the act of being and the essence, as inner principles of each existent. It is only an inquiry about two logically distinct aspects under which the concrete existent may be considered. For them, existence and quiddity are two determinations which differ only conceptually, not really.

It is evident, then, that the two elements which both doctrines distinguish in every existent are conceived in quite different manners. For the Suarezian, existence is nothing but the factual state of existing, of being posited, of being real, as contrasted with mere possibility. Such existence has no content, no positive determination, no grade of perfection in being. All of this is contributed only by the essence or quiddity, by that which is rendered real by existence. Hence even before it exists, while it is in the state of mere possibility, the existent is already fully determined, it has only to be transferred from the state of possibility into the state of actuality. The essence is not merely, as for the Thomists, an empty structural principle of that which this existent is, but the concrete positive determination of all that which it is. Whereas the Thomists claim that the whole positive content, the degree of perfection in being, derives from being as the principle of all positivity, the Suarezians attribute it to the essence, to which existence only adds the state of actuality or of reality. The difference shows even in the terminology. The Thomists speak of *esse* and *essentia,* the act of being and the principle of potentiality by which it is limited. The Suarezians speak of *existentia* and *quidditas,* the mere state of existing and the concrete determinations which may be transferred into this state.

We might perhaps say that both the Suarezian and the Thomistic distinction apply to all beings, that the former constitutes a first step which should naturally lead to the latter. We may first, with the Suarezians, consider every existent from the two logically distinct points of view of existence and whatness. Next, however, we must look into the existent's ontological structure, into the conditions of the possibility of such a distinction. The mistake of Suarezianism is to stop too soon. The Suarezian concept of existence should lead naturally to the concept of being as *act of being,* as we have tried to show above. We have seen that being cannot be understood as anything but the inner ground of every existent, through which it is posited in all its positive determinations.

Essence as Principle of Limitation

When we inquire, *What is this?,* we know that *this* is, but we do not yet know *what* it is. The fact that we ask about what it is supposes that we know already that it is a certain *what,* whereby it differs from the whatness of other things. If it differs in this way, that which it is contrasts with that which it is not. Hence existents possess being but not to its fullest extent, only within determined limits. That through which the existent is that which it is is its essence. Essence is that through which an existent is posited in a determined, limited manner of being.

(1) Whereas the act of being is the principle of all positivity in every existent, its essence is the principle of negativity, of limitation. Essence implies a negation of being, not a negation which suppresses the being of the existent and reduces it to nothing, but a negation which limits its being and reduces it to a finite being. It is not a total or absolute, but a partial and relative negation, which refers to certain determinations and denies their presence in this existent. Such a relative negation is also a negative relation, as it refers one existent to all others and distinguishes it from them. A relative negation is always a determined negation. It is determined by that to which it refers. Hence finiteness is always and necessarily determined finiteness. The finite existent is always and necessarily posited within limited and limiting determinations. Therefore, since the essence is that through which the existent is that which it is, and since, on the other hand, the finite existent is limited in its being and determined in its limitation, we must conceive of essence as of the principle of the limitation and determination of the existent.

(2) The finite existent is not the infinite, it is not absolute being. Through its essence it is opposed in negative relation to infinite being and thus is posited as finite. Hence the essence is the principle of the limitation of the existent, inasmuch as, in the negative relation to the unlimited, it posits the relative negation of the unlimited, thus distinguishing the existent from unlimited being and establishing it as finite.

But every finiteness is determined finiteness. The existent is not only limited in being, it is also determined in this limitation. It is *only* (limitation) *this* (determination). The relative opposition of the finite existent to unlimited being explains its limitation, not its determination. To unlimited being an indefinite number of limited beings may be opposed. It is another aspect of the essence which posits the finite existent in this determined way, making it different from all other existents and presupposing all the others not as real, but as possible.

(3) Hence the essence distinguishes the existent from unlimited being by limiting it and from all other existents by determining it. But what is this essence in itself? It is not being itself. For being is the principle of positivity, it has no limits, it implies no negation, it posits no difference. It cannot be the principle of limitation, and even less of determined limitation.

Nor can the essence be an existent. For such an existent could bring about a limitation only if it were itself a limited, determined existent, and this supposes a further existent to explain limitation. We would end up in an infinite regression, which explains nothing.

If neither being nor an existent can limit and determine the existent, it looks as if nothingness should do it, but certainly not mere nothingness or the negation of being as such. If the existent were limited by absolutely nothing, it would not be limited, it would simply be unlimited. Hence the principle of limitation is not absolute nothingness, but relative nothingness, nothingness not as absolute negation, but as relative negation of being, that is, as negation of certain determinations of being.

This negation does not refer to being or to the determinations of the existent itself, but only to further possible determinations which are negated of this existent. These negated determinations, however, are not simply negated, but rather positively presupposed. For a limit always separates from something. Hence the essence as principle of limitation and determination of the existent presupposes positively other determinations which are excluded from the existent or denied of it.

That which is thus excluded and denied is presupposed at least as possible. By excluding and denying it, the existent establishes itself positively in the possibility of limited determinations. Hence ultimately essence is the *determined and limited possibility of the existent.* It stands half-way between being and not-being. It neither causes the existent to be nor suppresses its existence, but it is presupposed by the being of this existent and provides it with the possibility of being this and not that. It outlines the pattern or structure of this determined existent.

(4) The essence as potentiality is not itself something which *is,* it is not an existent. It is finite as the essence of a finite being, but it is not finite in itself as an existent. It is not itself a finite existent. Hence we should not ask what limits the essence, since the question supposes that the essence is an existent. Essence as potentiality is neither the mere positivity of being nor the mere negativity of non-being, but rather something which stands between the two of them as relativity, that is, as the relative non-being of the possibility, as opposed to the reality of being.

However, as possibility of being, the essence cannot be something which would pre-exist to the actuality of the existent as ontically prior, having a reality all by its own. Such a conception makes of the essence an existent, a thing, a positivity which subsists in itself. The essence is nothing but an inner principle of the existent whose essence it is. It is absorbed into the existent as a constitutive ground, it exists only in and through the existent. But as a principle in this sense it is, in the unity of the existent, presupposed as ontologically previous to the reality of the existent, as it outlines for the latter a determined limited possibility of being and separates it from other possibilities.

85

The Difference Between Act of Being and Essence

(1) This difference is first a *logical* one, a difference between two different contents of our mind. The concept of *act of being* does not include the concept of *essence*. The being of the existent does not conceptually include its whatness: for it is not strictly the being of *this* existent but the being of beings in general. On the other hand, the essence or whatness of the existent does not conceptually imply its being.

If, however, we inquire about the metaphysical constitution of the existent, our question refers not to logically distinct aspects but to really distinct components, to the inner principles through which the real is constituted as such. When we showed that the existent's formal principle of reality was the act of being and that of its limitation the essence, we meant a *real difference*, between act of being and essence, a distinction which exists independently of and previous to our thinking of it. Being is really the ground of the reality of the existent, and the positive perfection of the finite existent is really limited to certain determinations. Hence the act of being and the essence are constitutive principles in the real order of the existent, not merely in the logical order of our concepts.

(2) Yet the act of being and the essence are not beings, but principles of being. Thus the difference between the two of them is not the same as that which exists between real beings. A real difference between beings may be called an *ontic difference*. It implies that the two terms exist independently as beings and may continue to exist even if separated from each other. The difference between the act of being and the essence is not of this kind. It is one not between beings, but between principles of being, which cannot subsist independently of each other. We may call it an *ontological difference,* because it proceeds beyond

86

the existent (*on*) to its ground or principle (*logos*). It implies that the members are really different, that one is really not the other, yet that neither can subsist by itself as an autonomous existent. As principles of being, they subsist only in that of which they are the principles, the existent itself. Hence the distinction between the act of being and the essence is a real difference, not, however, an ontic but an ontological difference. The Suarezians were right when they rejected a real ontic distinction between being and essence, but they were wrong when they did not admit a real ontological difference between the two of them.

(3) Heidegger has introduced the expression *ontological difference* as a way of indicating the difference between beings and being, between the ontic realm and the ontological realm. We believe that, underlying this difference between beings and being, there is one between the act of being and the essence. The difference between beings and being supposes another difference, which explains why the existent is not absolutely being itself and does not exhaust being in its totality, but is distinct from it as a determined limited realization of it. The difference between being and the existent demands in the latter a principle of the difference, the essence. Essence itself differs from being and communicates this difference to the existent whose essence it is. Hence the essence is the condition of the possibility of the ontological difference.

The Common Origin of Being and Essence

Being and essence can come together, determine each other, and thus bring about the existent only if they derive both from a common origin. Two really different and formally opposed principles cannot come together in a common unity if they do

87

not possess some previous unity, if they do not derive from a common source.

(1) This common unity might lie either in being, or in the essence, or in some other reality. But it cannot lie in some other reality, since such a reality, in order to exist, would have to consist of being and essence. Neither can it be the essence. The positivity of being cannot be rooted in the relativity or relative negativity of the essence.

On the other hand, the relativity of the essence may be rooted in the positivity of being, its potentiality may derive from actuality. Hence being is not rooted in essence, but essence is rooted in being. The essence is a determined manner of being, a possibility of being in finite realization. But such a manner or possibility must be rooted in being itself, insofar as being must provide the norm for whatever kind of form it may assume. Hence the common unity of being and essence lies necessarily in being.

(2) But how can the pure actuality of being bring forth its negation, the potentiality of the essence? If essence derives from being, it presupposes being. As principle of the essence, being must be previous to it. But being as the inner principle of the existent to which the essence belongs does not precede the essence. It is posited in the existent together with the essence as the real being of this existent. From such a being the essence cannot derive, since it is rather presupposed by it. Neither can the essence derive from the being which is the inner principle of other existents, since this being too is posited in its degree by some essence.

Hence the being in which the possibility of all finite essences is rooted can only be being itself, which is previous to all possible finite beings: *absolute being,* as the fullness of all possibilities of being. Hence if the finite essence as possibility of being derives from being as actuality of being, all finite essences as finite possibilities of being must derive from absolute being as the unlimited actuality of being, which precedes and gives rise to the finite duality of being and essence.

(3) But how can the empty potentiality of limited essences derive from the pure unlimited actuality of being? An answer to this question can be found only in the relativity in which the finite, limited being is constituted. If the finite essence is to derive from absolute being, relativity, as a constitutive element of the essence, must be posited in absolute being, without impairing its absolute identity. If absolute being is the first origin of all the multiplicity and diversity of the finite beings, it must, as absolute identity, contain at the same time difference or non-identity. This non-identity does not suppress the identity, but presupposes it and derives from it. This difference must be such that it does not introduce into the absolute positivity any negativity which might render the infinite finite, the absolute relative.

This is possible only if there is posited in the unity of absolute being a relative opposition, on account of which there may originate in it the essence of the finite existent. But we have already said that there exists such a relative difference in absolute being, insofar as it is absolute knowledge or self-knowledge, absolute identity of being and knowing. For in the act of knowledge the knower sets the known up against itself, although between the two of them there exists a perfect identity. If the finite essence is to originate in the identity of the absolute, there must exist in this identity a difference by which the finite possibility of being sets itself up against the absolute actuality of being. Such a difference can exist in the identity of the absolute without suppressing it, only if it is posited in the activity of knowing. In other words, absolute being must in its absolute knowledge oppose to itself the finite as the object of its knowledge. Insofar as it is opposed to the absolute, it is finite, projected, and established in its possibility by the absolute itself. Thus there originates in the absolute identity, in relative difference from it, the possibility of the finite existent. Likewise, there originates, again in the identity of the absolute, through the relative opposition of finite possibilities, the several determinations of the finite existent.

(4) This derivation of the finite existent from absolute being cannot be deduced or understood *a priori.* It can only be shown reductively. Hence we did not start from absolute being, but from the question. The question implies finiteness, finiteness implies essence. Essence must ultimately derive from absolute being. We have tried to show how this might be possible.

2. BEING AND ACTIVITY

Activity as Self-Actuation

Hitherto we have understood the existent through its inner constitution of being and essence. But we still do not know the existent completely in that which it is. This too we discover in the activity of inquiring. When we inquire what the existent is, the very act of inquiring provides an answer which proceeds beyond the existent as understood hitherto. Inquiring is an activity and this activity is neither our being nor our essence, since we *are* and we are *this* or *that* even if we do not carry out this activity. It is something else, and we must find out what it is.

In the act of inquiring we know ourself as a finite existent and as self-actuating, hence not only statically, as a "subject in itself," previous to any activity, but also dynamically, as a "subject in activity." This activity, as a second level of reality, proceeds above and beyond our being as our first level of reality. But this reality posited by our act derives from ourself. The existent actuates itself and through this self-actuation posits itself into a new reality which goes beyond its being and its essence. We call this reality *activity*. It is that wherein the existent by itself, proceeding beyond its own original being and essence, actuates itself and posits itself upon a new and higher level of reality. Activity is the self-actuation, the self-realization of the acting subject. Only in activity do the possibilities of the existent become full reality. Hence activity is not first and foremost the realization of objective possibilities, chosen by us as goal of our action, but the realization of the active subject himself, who transforms the possibilities of his essence into full reality.

Since activity appears to be a new element to be added to being and essence, proceeding beyond them through a new reality, we shall have to investigate the mutual relationship of the triad of *being, essence,* and *activity.*

Being as Principle of Activity

How is activity possible? Is the being of the existent not definitively limited by its essence, and is its essence not definitively realized by its act of being? How then is activity, as a further self-realization of the existent, still possible?

(1) Every activity is a new reality of the existent which raises the latter to a higher level of being. This reality derives from the existent itself—not, however, from its essence, which is the principle of limitation. Thus it derives from its act of being, which is the principle of its reality. It follows that the being of the existent is not wholly and definitively held within

91

certain limits by its essence. Being, even when limited by essence, must possess potentialities which break through these limits. It is endowed with a dynamism which is capable of raising the existent from its first level of reality to a higher one.

(2) Although in the finite existent being is limited by essence, it remains *being*. But of and by itself being is unconditioned and unlimited. The limitation imposed upon it by the essence is contrary to its nature; it is a self-alienation of being, through which it no longer is what it is of and by itself. That is why being tries to break through the limitation and to reach its own unlimited fullness.

(3) In the finite existent being is limited by the finite essence. But it remains being, principle of unlimited actuality. As being of the finite existent it is *actually finite*, but as simply being it is *virtually infinite*. Therefore, insofar as the self-actuation of the finite existent is a self-actuation of being, it transcends the limits of the existent towards the fullness of actuality, although this occurs only in the manner and within the range which is possible to a finite existent.

We have here a dialectic between being, essence, and activity. Being is the immediacy of pure positivity and self-identity. Essence is the mediation as negativity and non-identity of being with itself. Activity is mediated immediacy as a new positivity which "sublates" the negativity, as a new self-identity which "sublates" the non-identity. But if activity is the third, synthetic element, the positivity of being mediated by the negativity of the essence, it follows that activity is determined not only by being, but also by the essence. Activity derives from the unity of being and essence. This brings up the two following questions: How is the activity determined by the essence of the existent? And how are being and essence united in activity?

Essence as Principle of Activity

Activity derives from the existent, which is constituted of being and essence. Hence activity too is determined not only by being, but also by the essence of the existent. Being, as the principle of actuality, explains why the existent in its activity breaks through the limitation of its essence; and the essence, as the principle of limitation, explains why the activity itself is limited by the possibilities of each existent. It explains the finiteness of the existent not only in its being, but also in its activity. Although the dynamism of the activity derives from the virtual infinity of being, the activity of the finite being remains always restricted in actual finiteness; it can never reach the full actuality of being. How, then, does the essence exert its influence upon the activity?

Activity is the self-actuation of the existent, through which it posits itself beyond the limits of its essence in a new reality. But when it puts itself thus in a new reality, which stands outside its own limited being, it is no longer strictly speaking *its own* reality, but *another* reality, that is, the reality of the other. In other words, it actuates itself into otherness, it reaches a new reality, it realizes itself in its otherness. Thus we may say that finite activity is the self-actuation of the existent in its other, in that which is not itself, through which it posits the other's reality as its own. However, the essence is not only relation, but also negation. Therefore, the existent must not only actuate itself by turning into its other, it must also set itself up over against the other, thus positing itself in its own determined and limited reality.

As a result, there is this strange dialectic: it is only through activity that the existent actuates itself and posits itself in its own limited reality. At the same time, its activity puts it on a level which transcends its own essence. The existent posits itself within its limit by actively transcending this limit. It is only by going beyond the limit that the limit is posited. The essence of the existent is realized only if, through its activity, it reaches beyond its essence. The existent cannot statically subsist within its limited actuality; it is always dynamically reaching beyond it. *Of its very nature every being is active.*

Substance and Accident

(1) Insofar as the existent is originally posited by the two principles of being and essence, it is traditionally called *substance*. Any further reality which accrues to the substance, surpassing and further determining it, is called *accident*. Activity, and to some extent only activity, is such a reality which surpasses and further determines the substance. Hence activity is the basic accident, which we discover first, and from which other accidents may be deduced.

(2) What is meant, more precisely, by substance and accident? The existent is originally constituted by its act of being and its essence. It is posited as a limited, but real, being, as something which exists in itself, autonomously, as a substance. Being in itself is the essence of substance; it is in itself, not merely in another. Activity, on the other hand, exists as the activity of the substance, produced by the substance. It is, it is an existent, but it is not autonomous, it does not exist in itself. It exists in another, it is not a being-in-itself but a being-in-another, and this is the essential characteristic of the accident.

(3) It follows that the existent, the being in the first and original sense, is the substance. The accident too is really a being, but in a secondary and derivative sense. It follows further that every being is either substance or accident, for it either is in

itself or in another. Finally, it follows that a finite substance can never exist without accident, for every being must act, and this acting is an accident.

Every being acts, the substance necessarily carries some accident. But what kind of accident it must carry is not determined. From this necessity of acting and from the non-necessity of this or that determined acting, derives the possibility of change; or, as the ancients said, of movement (*kinèsis, motus*) in the finite substance.

3. THE LAWS OR PRINCIPLES OF BEING

The Principle of Identity

(1) Whenever we inquire about a being, we know, before any answer is given, that it is what it is, that it cannot be something else than what it is. Without this kind of knowledge no answer could be given to our question. Inquiring and knowing presuppose this pre-knowledge of the necessary identity of every being. Every being is necessarily itself; this is the *principle of identity*. A negative but equivalent formulation is: A being cannot not be itself. This is the *principle of contradiction*.

(2) This principle is at times expressed in the formula: $A = A$. The formula is correct, but insufficient, for it is a mere tautology which does not express the whole meaning of the principle. We must rather say: A necessarily is A. This formula shows that the principle of identity is neither a tautology nor a purely analytical statement, but a *synthetic statement*, whose predicate contains more than the subject: the necessity for every being of being itself, the impossibility of it being something else. This formula also shows that in this *ontic* formulation (as applied to single beings) the principle is based upon another,

95

upon an *ontological* law (applying to being itself). That which is simple necessary and necessarily identical with itself is not every single being, but only being. To the ontic formula we must add: *insofar as it is.*

Thus the *principle of ontic identity* states: Insofar as a being is, it is necessarily. Or, negatively: Insofar as a being is, it cannot not be. The *principle of ontological identity* states: Being necessarily is being. Negatively stated: Being cannot not be.

The Principle of Causality

(1) Whenever we inquire or know, we know that a being, insofar as it is, is necessarily itself. It is necessarily, but only if and insofar as it IS, only under the condition that it is posited in and by being. Hence every being is both conditioned and unconditioned. Further, we affirm the conditioned unconditionally, the conditioned must be posited into the *unconditionality* of being. Otherwise, the conditioned would by itself, through its own essence, be both conditioned and unconditioned, which is contradictory. Hence in order to be grasped without contradiction, every being requires some positive element, by which it is posited into the unconditionality of being, through which it is rendered as unconditional as being. It requires a *ground,* a *sufficient reason* of its being.

(2) We may put it in another way. Every being is both necessary and not necessary. It is not necessary, insofar as it is a finite being, which is not by itself, through its own essence, determined to the necessity of being. But if it is, it is as necessary as being; then, insofar as it is, it can no longer not be. Insofar as it is, it necessarily is. This is possible only if every being, over and above its own contingent essence, possesses something which determines it to the necessity of being. Else it would

by itself be both necessary and not necessary, which is contradictory. Therefore, every contingent being which is, which is posited in the necessity of being, requires a positive element, by which it is determined to the necessity of being: it requires a ground, a sufficient reason of its being.

Contingent beings do not have the ground of their being in themselves. But if they require a ground and if this ground is not in themselves, it must lie in some other being, it must be an outside or exterior ground. Hence they are posited into being by something else. But to bring forth some reality which goes beyond one's own being and essence is to act. Hence the contingent being is the product of the activity of some other being. Its exterior cause is an *efficient* cause, a cause which actively brings it about. It follows that every contingent being which is, is necessarily posited into being by an efficient cause. This is the law of the cause or the *principle of causality*.

(3) The principle of causality cannot be established through analytic deduction but only through synthetic reduction. It is not formally contained in the principle of identity and it cannot be deduced from it. The principle is one more example of mediated immediacy: it is immediately evident, but it can be critically established only through the mediation of the dynamism of our intellect, by which we are irresistibly urged to look beyond every being to the ground or cause of its being. Let us see how that is so.

(4) We know that, whenever a being is, it necessarily is. It is necessarily on account of being. Being is the reason, the sufficient reason of its necessity. We may formulate this truth in the *principle of sufficient reason:* Insofar as it is, every being necessarily has a sufficient reason. Our thinking takes place within the horizon of being as the ultimate and the unconditioned. On account of its dynamism it strives always and neces-

sarily, past every finite being, towards the ultimate and the un-conditioned, towards being as the ground and sufficient reason of every being. Thus some knowledge of being as the sufficient reason of every being is always already unthematically co-posited, as a condition of its very possibility, in every act of inquiring and of knowing.

(5) The being of the finite and contingent existent is its ultimate and unconditioned element, the *inner* ground of its unconditioned reality. But is is not absolutely ultimate and un-conditioned, since it is a contingent being, conditionally un-conditioned, not necessarily necessary. Since our thinking irre-sistibly strives towards the ultimate and the unconditioned, it passes necessarily beyond every being towards the ground of its reality. This ground is not this being itself, insofar as it is con-ditioned. Hence another ground is required, which determines every being to be: a positing or efficient cause. Thus we have formulated the *principle of causality:* Contingent being is brought about by a cause. This is an application of the universal principle of sufficient reason to the being of the contingent being.

This principle is unthematically co-posited and co-affirmed in every act of inquiring or of knowing. Since our thinking occurs against the horizon of the ultimate and of the unconditioned, it strives towards being as the ground of each being, it strives towards the last and unconditioned ground: absolute being.

(6) It might be useful to explain briefly the relation which exists between the notions of ground, sufficient reason, condition, and cause. In general, the ground is that through which some-thing is or is posited. Sufficient reason, as used in the expression, "the principle of sufficient reason," is used in English and in other languages as an equivalent of the German word *Grund.* We may use it as a synonym of *ground.* It has an epistemological

connotation, as contrasted with the more ontological connotation of *ground*. A *condition* is that which underlies the *possibility* of a being: it is that which must be so that something else may be *possible*. Every ground is a condition, but not every condition is a ground. No real difference is required between the ground and that which is posited by it: absolute being is to itself the ground of its own being. When there is a distinction between the two of them, the ground may also be called a *cause*. Hence the ground is that through which *something* is, the cause is that through which *something else* is.

(7) We may further distinguish between *inner* or *intrinsic causes* and *outer* or *extrinsic causes*. The act of being and the essence are inner causes of a being. When they are present, the being exists. We have seen above that the intrinsic causes are not sufficient to explain the reality of the finite being. It requires also extrinsic causes. The first of these is the *efficient cause*, whose essence it is to posit something else through its activity. We shall later consider two other extrinsic causes, the *final cause* and the *exemplary cause*.

Finally, a distinction may be made between the *primary or first cause* and the *secondary causes*. Being is the primary cause; being alone can posit a being as being. But the finite beings can also produce certain effects; they are secondary causes, whose causality is dependent on the causality of the primary and universal cause.

The Principle of Finality

(1) Whenever we inquire about something we inquire *in order* to know. But inquiring is an activity. We call that which an activity intends its end, purpose, or goal. Hence some specific knowledge is the purpose of the inquiry. The act of inquiring

really intends a goal, otherwise the question would be impossible. But when we inquire about something, our question implies that we can know it. Hence in the act of questioning we presuppose that we can reach through knowledge that about which we inquire and on account of which we inquire. We presuppose that we can realize the purpose of our activity. The possibility of this realization is a condition of the possibility of our inquiring activity.

However, the movement of inquiring is not at an end when it has reached some particular being. Since this being is conditioned by the horizon of being against which it is posited, it is not yet fully grasped when it is known only as what it is; it should be known in the totality in which it is situated. The dynamism of our intellect pushes irresistibly, although unthematically, past every finite being towards its ultimate ground, towards being as the unconditioned horizon. Hence the movement of our mind always intends absolute being. This striving, this finality is co-affirmed, as a condition of its possibility, in every act of thinking. And every single object, which is known as a being, is grasped as a partial end or goal, as a step towards unlimited being. It follows that every single being, as such, is essentially subordinated to absolute being, since it is used by our mind as a step or a means towards it.

(2) What is true of the activity of inquiring, is true of all activity. Whenever a finite being acts, it actuates itself in a new manner, which goes beyond its own being and essence and enriches it with a new reality and perfection. Activity is a self-actuation and self-realization of the existent. Hence every existent acts in order to establish itself in a new reality and perfection, in order to actuate and to realize itself. But that which is intended by an activity is its purpose or goal. If therefore every being acts only because and insofar as, through its activity, it puts itself into a new reality, which is the end or purpose of its

100

activity, we may formulate the following principle: Whenever a being acts, it acts for a certain end or goal. This is the *principle of finality*. Insofar as the end intended influences the activity, by inducing the agent to perform it and by giving it a direction, it is the ground or the cause of this activity, it is its final cause.

(3) But the purpose of activity is not only the self-actuation of the agent, but also—and even more basically—the actuation of being as such. The being's activity is possible only because its being, although it is limited by its essence, breaks through this limit and establishes it on a higher level of reality. But when being proceeds in this way beyond the limits of essence, it does not set itself up, as being, within a new limit; it strives rather towards the full actuation of the identity of being as such. Being is dynamic self-identity; this is the condition of the possibility and the reason of the necessity of all finite activity. Because being is dynamic identity, every being must act and all activity is purposive. Through its activity every being endeavors to reach the pure self-identity of being. This is the final purpose or end of all activity. But since activity is tied to the limited possibilities of the finite essence, no finite being can reach this end immediately in its totality; immediately, it can only posit specific limited realities. These are partial ends, which are subordinated to the final and necessary end of all activity: the actuation of being as such.

(4) Every activity is necessarily purposive, whether it be directed by a conscious knowledge of the purpose (formal finality) or deriving from the unconscious natural necessity of the agent (material finality). Even in the latter case there is real finality, since acting as such is possible only on the basis of a previous determination of the end. We have tried to establish this fact by an examination of the nature of activity as the self-

101

actuation or self-realization of the finite agent. However, we do not mean to say that, in some kinds of activity, especially in material activity, the act may not intend a reality which is distinct from that of the agent. The activity may intend another being and lose itself in it. In this case, the goal itself does not coincide with the activity which intends it. The other reality, intended by such an activity, may not exist as yet and may have to be produced by the activity itself; or it may already exist, and only be assimilated by the activity. Yet even in the latter case something must be produced, namely, the activity of the agent. Even when the activity loses itself in another being, this is possible only because and insofar as the reality of the other is the reality of the agent itself, because and insofar as the agent actuates and realizes itself in its own reality only by acting upon the other and losing itself in it.

IV.

BEING AND SPIRIT

THE act of inquiring has shown that the inquirer is a finite being. This information allowed us to deduce the inner constitution of the finite being as such. A finite being is that which it is through the act of being and the essence. But inquiring or the question was not yet fully explained. Inquiring is an act, which proceeds beyond the first level of the being and puts it on a higher level. This explanation enabled us to deduce the essence of activity and to show its relation to being and essence, but it too does not wholly explain inquiring. Inquiring is an activity, but not every activity is an inquiry. Thus that which is posited in the act of inquiring and unthematically known in it, leads us beyond the object of thematic knowledge. It forces us to continue reflecting, thus revealing ever new contents. Our next task is to understand the question as an activity of the spiritual existent, to derive from it the essence of the spirit, as it keeps actuating itself, against the horizon of the world and of being, towards absolute being.

1. SPIRIT IN SELF-ACTUATION

The Question as Actuation of Being

(1) When we inquire about something, we know about ourself and about something different from ourself. We actuate ourself as the subject of the inquiry; we posit ourself as subject

in act, which presupposes that we exist as subject in itself; at the same time, we posit an object in act and we presuppose it as object in itself.

Hence the question is a self-actuation of the inquirer. But it is a self-actuation, in which the inquirer passes beyond himself towards something other, insofar as he makes of this other the object of his inquiry and of his knowing. In this sense, the question is an actuation of the other, of the object of the inquiry by the inquirer. In all of this it is one and the same actuation, which embraces the difference of subject and object. It posits the difference of subject and object and it presupposes this difference.

(2) The act of inquiring is an act of knowledge. But all knowledge is knowledge about being. When we inquire, we know that we ourself, the inquirer, are posited as being. This knowledge is an accident or second actuation, enriching our substantial, primary actuation, through which we are ourself. It is therefore a *self-actuation in being,* in the fullest sense of the word. It reaches the things not from a particular or restricted point of view, but in that which they are really in themselves. It reaches beings in their being, under the form or formal object of being. Such an activity stands necessarily in the horizon of being as such, which encompasses all beings as beings.

Hence, when in our knowledge we actuate the other, this too is an actuation in being. It is *an actuation of the other in being.* But self-actuation and the actuation of the other coincides in my knowledge. This does not mean that our substantial, primary being coincides with the primary being of the other; it means that our accidental, secondary being, our activity as a knower coincides with the secondary, accidental being of the other.

Spiritual Actuation and Consciousness

(1) The question is an actuation, in which the inquirer posits himself as subject and the other as object of the question, as he actuates both of them under the form of being and within the horizon of being. But an actuation which actuates beings under the form of being and within the horizon of being is what we call a *spiritual actuation*. Insofar as it reaches being as being, it posits its identity with being as being. But such an identity of the actuation with being as being is knowledge. Hence it is an actuation of knowledge, an actuation which knows itself—an actuation in which a being possesses and actuates itself in knowing self-presence, under the form of being. But if it actuates itself in knowledge under the form of being, it actuates itself in the horizon of being as such, it is enabled to actuate in knowledge, under the form of being, other things which *are*.

(2) Thus we understand the nature of consciousness. We call *conscious activity* an activity which knows itself, which possesses itself in knowledge, which is present to itself. This self-luminosity has its basis in the original identity of being and knowing in our knowing activity, it derives from self-consciousness. Insofar as it is a knowing under the form of being and within the horizon of being, it is a knowledge which is able to reach out for the other, so that the other as other enters the *light* of consciousness, always, however, in the formal identity of being. This is consciousness of the object.

The Nature of the Finite Spirit

(1) The act of inquiring has revealed to us the nature of conscious spiritual activity. It is the self-actuation of a being in the light of being and within the horizon of being, always reaching

105

out beyond itself to the unlimited totality of being as such. This is precisely the nature of the *spirit*. The spirit is a being characterized by the power to actuate itself consciously, that is, as knowing being, in the light and the horizon of being as such. However, a spirit that cannot grasp being in its fullness, but always only as the being of a finite being, is a *finite spirit*.

(2) This power and limitation explains the inner tension in the nature of the finite spirit. The finite spirit can be understood only through the opposition of finiteness and infinity, for, insofar as it is spirit, it actuates itself and the other really in the horizon of being as a whole. It reaches out towards being as a whole in a mixture of knowing and not-knowing. As a spirit, the finite spirit reaches out towards the infinity of being. But as finite, the finite spirit can never catch up with the infinite range of the horizon of being. This horizon remains forever at an infinite distance from it. Hence the infinity of the finite spirit is not that of actual possession, but the *virtual infinity* of reaching out; but its being and activity are confined within *actual finiteness*.

2. SPIRIT AND HORIZON

The Finite Spirit and its Object

The act of inquiring has brought out the duality of subject and object, not only in the sense that subject and object are opposed to each other in this act, but also in the sense that they are opposed to each other in themselves. Every act of consciousness refers to some other reality. This is a basic fact of inner experience. We know about ourself only while knowing about the other. Self-awareness presupposes awareness of the other.

We shall try to show that this presupposition follows *a priori* from the very essence of the finite spirit.

(1) The finite spirit knows being as being, that is, it grasps itself and others in the light and in the horizon of being. Yet it never grasps being as such, in its totality. It knows about being only while knowing about beings. These beings are limited, they are *this* or *that* being. Hence the finite spirit knows about being only while knowing *what* a finite being is, only while knowing about the essence, the whatness of beings.

This applies also to the self-knowledge of the spirit. When we know about ourself *that* we are, we must also, to some extent, although unthematically, know *what* we are. No clear, exhaustive knowledge is required, but only some vague and implicit knowledge of our own nature.

(2) We know ourself as a *finite being,* that is, as a being but not as being itself. This supposes that from the start we somehow distinguish being as such from our own being. It supposes that we are aware, however unthematically, of the *difference* between being and our own being, of the *transcendence* of being with respect to our own being.

Hence we must know ourself as limited, we must be aware of a limit as limit. However, awareness of a limit as limit supposes that we know about something beyond the limit. This something cannot be transcendent being as a whole, for, as a finite being, we cannot grasp being as a whole, but only the being of a finite existent. Therefore, we can know about being beyond our own being only in finite existents which we are not ourself, that stand outside of us as the other. Only by *knowing of the other* as other can we know of the difference and transcendence of being with respect to our own being. Only by knowing of this difference and transcendence can we know of our own finiteness and limitation. Since we can never

107

know at all without at least implicitly knowing about our own finiteness, it follows that knowledge of the other is required for all self-knowledge. It is a condition of the latter's possibility.

(3) There is a *reciprocal relation* between knowing about ourselves and knowing about the other. Either of them is conditioned by the other. For we can know the other as being only if we know about being, which we do only in and through an act of self-awareness. And we have seen that knowing about ourself presupposes knowing about the other.

The relation is reciprocal, although not from the same point of view. In order to know the other *as being* we must first know about ourself; in order to know of ourself as a *finite being* we must know of the other. In other words, we know of being as such only in the *identity* of our own act of knowledge. And we know of the *difference* between our own being and being as such only through our knowledge of the other as other. Or again, we are aware of our own being in our act of self-knowledge, and we are aware of our own essence through our knowledge of the other.

The Horizon of Being and the Horizon of the World

The finite spirit knows itself only through the mediation of the other. This other cannot be the horizon of being as a whole; in order to know this horizon the spirit would have to be infinite. For the same reason, the other cannot be immediately the being of God. The other from which the finite spirit distinguishes itself in order to be aware of itself can only be something which, it can know immediately as its object. This object can only be some other finite being or a collection of such beings. Thus we see how within the *universal horizon of being* (its adequate object) there stands out for the finite spirit a special partial horizon (its proportionate object), which we may call the *world horizon* or simply the world.

In this sense, then, the world is not a sum total of beings, much less the sum total of the beings which the finite spirit happens to know. Rather, it is that whole range of beings, connected *a priori* with the essence of the finite spirit, which may for the latter become possible objects of knowledge.

The Immediacy of the World

Since the finite spirit needs the mediation of the other in order to reach self-awareness, and since this other necessarily is a being in the world, it follows that the finite spirit possesses an immediate certitude of the world. This certitude does not have to refer to any single particular object. It is enough that the spirit should know of a world of beings which exists really all around itself.

Hence all attempts to demonstrate the outside world by means of the principle of causality should be rejected. The mediate character of such a demonstration contrasts strongly with the immediacy of our certitude about the world. Although a mediate philosophical proof may come up to the level of a pre-reflexive immediate certitude, it seems better to make the immediate certitude fully reflexive and to justify it.

What is to be "demonstrated" is not an ontic state of affairs, but a transcendental necessity, not the existence of a world of things in themselves, but the *a priori* necessity of the immediate certitude of such a world. Hence we do not try to demonstrate mediately that this world "is" in itself, but we show transcendentally—from the nature of the self-actuation of a finite spirit—that in every act of consciousness we of necessity always already co-affirm the reality of the world outside of us. This does not transform the immediacy of this knowledge, as it

109

occurs in our ordinary awareness, into mediated knowledge. But it makes this knowledge transcendentally obvious in its *a priori* necessity, turning it thus into a *mediated immediacy*.

In every "demonstration" of the reality of the outside world the critique of knowledge presupposes assumptions of which it is not reflexively aware. A demonstration of the objective reality of the world is possible only because *a priori* the world stands open for us. Should this not be the case, we would not even be able to inquire about the existence or non-existence of the world; *a fortiori*, we would be unable to use a metaphysical principle, the principle of causality, for a proof. The critique of knowledge presupposes a metaphysical foundation and cannot supply this foundation for itself. As the fundamental science, metaphysics has to lay the foundation for itself and for all other sciences, including the right kind of critique of knowledge.

3. THE ANALOGY OF BEING

Dialectics as Analogy

Looking back upon the data gathered hitherto, we see in human knowledge a steady dynamism which assumes the form of a dialectical process. This dynamism proceeds beyond everything laid down in concepts. It discovers the conditioned and limited nature of knowledge, and in this awareness of the limit it reaches beyond the latter and pushes our thematic knowledge of being ever further and deeper. Our knowledge can never be wholly conceptualized, it never catches up with its ultimate term. This dialectics of our knowledge about being is traditionally called the *analogy* of being.

(1) Whenever we ask what something *is,* we answer: This is a being, that is a being. But this answer is insufficient, it gives

110

rise to new questions. Carried by our pre-knowledge of being as such, these questions proceed beyond every single being, beyond all conceptual knowledge about beings. The answer is not false, it is insufficient, it leads to further inquiry, which reveals further aspects of being. That which is thus revealed about being in the very act of questioning may be caught up in concepts and made thematic, yet it does not set an end to our questioning. It impels us to further inquiring and to deepening of our knowledge.

We have here a dialectic union between *concept and act*, or more precisely, between our thematic knowledge and our unthematic preconceptual knowledge which is posited in the act of knowing itself and proceeds beyond that which may be expressed in concepts. The concept is not refuted, but exceeded by the act. The dialectic is animated by being. *Analogy* is precisely such a dialectical movement in which every determination which has been reached is not cancelled out, but exceeded by another, thus revealing ever further aspects of being.

(2) Analogy may be interpreted statically and dynamically. Considered statically—that is, logically, conceptually—it means: When we grasp being as being, we grasp it in that through which it agrees with everything else, and also, at the same time, in that which distinguishes it from all the rest. In the general concept of *a being,* we grasp what is basically common to all beings, but we are unable to separate it clearly from the diversity of these beings, since the being of beings posits simultaneously what is common and what differs in them. But a general concept which means both what is common and what is proper to all beings, a concept which receives no further determinations from something else, but which determines itself, because, although one, it applies to the single cases in an essentially different sense,—such a concept is called an *analogous* concept.

111

In all of this we can see also the *dynamic aspect* of our analogous knowledge of being. When we assert of something that it is, our statement is true. But this being is affirmed in the horizon of being, our thematic knowledge of it never catches up with our unthematic knowledge of being as such. So we continue to inquire about being, we look for it in other existents which offer us more being. This dynamic and dialectical increase of our knowledge of being derives from the analogy of being. Because being is realized differently—analogously—our knowledge about being must grasp each being, while reaching out beyond every single one of them to other beings, and thus, ultimately, to being itself, as the final goal of all inquiring and knowing.

Analogous and Univocal Concepts

(1) When we know something as *a being,* we know it not under a partial, abstract point of view, but in its totality. We know other things too as beings, and they also are known in their totality under the same concept. Hence the concept of being, while remaining unchanged, is used in quite different senses when applied to different things. It is an *analogous* concept. Such a concept receives its further determinations not from something else, but from itself. Thus when we call man a rational being, the determination *rational* does not come to being from outside, for rationality is one aspect of being. Our concept simply makes explicit something which was already contained in being.

On the other hand, we understand by a *univocal* concept a concept which receives further concrete determinations from something else, which is neither explicitly nor implicitly contained in it, but comes to it from outside as a new and further specification. Thus when we speak of a rational animal, the term *rational* is not contained in the concept of *animal*, it adds something new to it; hence the term *animal* is a univocal concept.

(2) Univocal concepts presuppose the analogous concept of being as a condition of their possibility. A univocal universal concept is possible only because and insofar as it is abstract, as its content is well determined and shared by a plurality of individuals, while it overlooks the further determinations through which these individuals differ from each other. By further abstraction it is possible to rise to more general concepts with increasing extension and decreasing comprehension. Yet insofar as they abstract from all differentiating determinations, these concepts remain univocal concepts. In this direction of increasing abstraction it is not possible to reach an ultimate, all-encompassing unity. Of its nature the univocal concept supposes other determinations not included within itself. Otherwise, it would be unable to abstract from them. Hence univocal concepts necessarily presuppose a plurality of different contents which are separated from each other. At the same time, they suppose as a condition of their possibility that this plurality constitutes an ordered unity. This unity can no longer be univocal, it must be analogous. The ultimate, all-encompassing unity can no longer be further determined from "without" through something "else," since there no longer is any "without" nor anything "else." It can no longer, like a univocal concept, be differentiated through further determinations not contained within it but coming from outside. Rather, it must differentiate itself out of itself. Hence the ultimate unity which comprises all univocal concepts must of necessity be an analogical unity.

(3) Analogous concepts are sometimes interpreted as if they were intermediate between univocal and equivocal concepts.

113

Univocal concepts apply to their objects in the same sense, equivocal concepts apply to their objects in different senses. Analogous concepts apply to their objects partly in the same, partly in a different sense. Logically, this explanation is correct. It may, however, produce the impression that the analogous concept is a derivative, artificially constructed one, which tries to mediate between univocal and equivocal concepts. In fact, the analogous concept is the condition of possibility of conceptual thinking as such; it is presupposed by the univocal concepts rather than deriving from them. Without the ultimate, all-encompassing unity, all relations between concepts would utterly disappear, we would have conceptual chaos. This ultimate unity is no longer univocal, but analogous.

(4) The concept of being is analogous because it is transcendent, because a concept which comprises absolutely all reality cannot further be determined by anything else. Hence it is not quite correct to call the concept of being the *most abstract* of all concepts, the concept possessing the widest extension and the smallest comprehension. The concept of being abstracts from nothing, since all that from which it might abstract, all the concrete determinations of beings, are themselves being. Therefore, the concept of being is not the most abstract, but *the most concrete* of all concepts: since absolutely every reality is being, the concept of being comprises it unto its last concrete particularities.

The concept of being is abstract in the sense that it does not explicitly grasp the individual and concrete determinations of every being. But in this respect it differs essentially from the univocal concept. In the univocal concept, further determinations are contained neither explicitly nor implicitly. In the analogous concept, they are contained implicitly, although they are not yet grasped explicitly.

Analogy and the Horizon of Being

(1) In our acts of questioning and of knowing we grasp beings as beings. Since all determinations of beings are beings, our concept of beings contains not only an abstract aspect, but the full and concrete determination of every being. How is this possible?

The determinations of all beings cannot be contained formally in the concept of these beings; they are not constitutive but differentiating determinations, they do not make the things into beings, but into such or such beings. Their number is infinite, and only an infinite spirit can actually know them. Our spirit is actually finite, but virtually infinite. It follows that we cannot actually, but only *virtually,* know of all the possible determinations of all beings. In what sense?

(2) The virtual infinity of the finite spirit is the infinity of the horizon, within which our inquiring and knowing takes place and our knowledge of beings as beings occurs. Absolutely everything is comprised in this horizon, although not everything is grasped by us in actual knowledge. The horizon as such is not an actual content of our knowledge, it must be actualized and made concrete in our knowing activity. The infinite horizon of being can never be reached by any finite act of the human spirit; hence the human spirit never enjoys an exhaustive knowledge of being as a whole, it knows of being only when knowing of finite beings. However, the infinite horizon of being infinitely surpasses whatever the spirit knows in its finite acts of knowledge; that is why the dynamism of the spirit pushes ever further, in order to come nearer to a knowledge of being in its every act of knowledge about beings.

The virtual infinity of the concept of being is nothing but the infinite dynamism, the infinite virtuality of the finite spirit

115

itself, as, in every act of knowledge, it reaches out towards the infinity of its horizon.

The Analogy of Absolute Being

All inquiring and knowing occur in the horizon of being, which, as horizon, is constituted by absolute being. It follows that the latter can stand only in a relation of analogy to the finite beings within this horizon.

(1) If absolute being constitutes the horizon of being, it cannot itself be an object within this horizon. The knowledge of an object presupposes the all-encompassing horizon, since only within it are objects possible. Hence none of these objects can be the horizon.

Yet absolute being as horizon is not totally different from the objects within this horizon. We have seen that the finite spirit always and necessarily, in all its questioning and knowing, reaches out towards absolute being as to the absolute and absolutely necessary *whereunto* of its spiritual dynamism. But this would be impossible if the absolute should be something unreachably different from the finite, objective contents of our inquiring and knowing. It is possible only if the absolute—despite its essential difference from all finite beings—has ultimately something in common with them, if the contents of the objective innerworldly inquiring and knowing refer beyond themselves and, becoming transparent, make us know in the conditioned and finite beings of our experience the unconditioned and unlimited reality of absolute being.

(2) Thus we have explained the *analogy of absolute being* with respect to the finite beings, which is the basic form of all analogy. Absolute being too *is,* but not in the same way as

116

finite beings. It is the horizon of all beings and can therefore not be a being in this horizon. When we say that it *is*, the word *is* is used neither univocally nor equivocally with the *is* which we affirm of finite beings. It is used analogously.

Analogy as the Negation of the Negation

The question arises how we can reach absolute being through analogy. How can we have an analogous yet positive knowledge of absolute being?

(1) The finite being is not pure being, but being limited by essence. But when the finite spirit knows such finite being, it grasps the latter in the horizon of being as such. It is only because, in its spiritual activity, it always reaches for the infinite, beyond the limits of the finite, that it is able to know the limit as limit, the finite as finite, negativity as negativity, and that it succeeds in lifting the limitation of the finite in a *negation of the negation.* By overcoming the negativity of the limit, it is capable of grasping the positivity of pure being. Negation of the negation does not mean here a negation of any positive aspect of being, but only the negation of the negativity which limits the positive content of being, the negation of the limit as such. The result of this negation is pure position, pure affirmation, of pure being without any restriction.

(2) The beings we know are all finite. However, they are constituted by pure being and its limitation. If we abstract from this limitation we get once more concepts of pure being, which contain no more limit and lead our mind towards infinity. Since all these concepts are without limit, they are no longer separated from other similar concepts. They coincide one with another. And they all apply to the one unlimited reality,

117

absolute being. They apply to absolute being *formally,* that is, in their full and proper sense, although *eminently,* in a manner which exceeds infinitely the manner in which they apply to finite beings. Likewise, we have a *proper* concept of these pure perfections of being, insofar as we discover them realized in a finite manner in the limited beings and as we grasp them in their purity by abstracting from their limit. Yet we have only an *analogous* concept of the way in which they are realized, in their primordial purity, in the unity and infinity of absolute being. We always attain the infinite only in the dynamism of our spirit, striving beyond the finite towards the infinite, without ever being able to possess it statically in an ordinary concept. We always need the mediation of a negation of the negation, which can never be replaced by the immediacy of a pure position.

(3) It is at once evident that not all concepts may be thus applied to absolute being. In some of them the limitation is an essential element. They disappear as such if it is dropped. Other concepts contain no such limitation: they refer to pure perfections which happen to be limited in the finite being, but which remain unchanged if this limitation is dropped. What are these concepts, which we may apply to absolute being?

Absolute being is pure self-presence of being with itself. It is therefore absolute spirit. And all perfections which apply to the spirit as such may be predicated of absolute spirit. All that which, in the finite spirit, derives from the spirit in it, may be analogously applied to absolute spirit. On the other hand, whatever in the finite spirit derives from finiteness as such, cannot be attributed to infinite spirit. Hence being, spirit, activity, consciousness, and such other spiritual attributes as we shall discover later, may be analogously attributed in their formal sense to absolute being.

118

(4) Hegel claims that all perfections which are attributed to absolute being in an eminent way disappear into infinity and lose all determination. This objection derives from Spinoza's axiom that every determination is a negation. Drop the negation, and there is no more determination.

The objection applies to what is traditionally called *mixed* perfections, which contain a limitation or negation as a constitutive element. It does not apply, however, to the pure perfections to which a limitation may be added that is not essential to them. When we drop this limit, the meaning of such perfections is not destroyed, it is only driven into infinity. It is true that in absolute being such perfections all coincide with each other and with absolute being itself. Their distinction derives not from their absolute content but from the finite nature of our knowing.

V.

THE SELF-UNFOLDING OF BEING

WE have seen that every existent is posited in its being by its act of being and limited by its essence. Insofar as beings possess more or less being, they are analogous. However, there are certain aspects of being which necessarily go together with it and cannot be excluded by any kind of limitation. They are not restricted to any range of beings, they are transcendent like being itself. That is why they are known traditionally as the *transcendental properties* of being or simply as the *transcendentals*. They are the properties of oneness or unity, of truth and of goodness.

We shall once more consider the question as question and try to show that it implies the three above mentioned properties of being as conditions of its very possibility.

1. BEING AS UNITY

Being as Principle of Unity

(1) We may inquire about everything. But this is possible only if we do not have to inquire about everything in particular, if we may inquire about everything at once. This supposes, however, that everything constitutes a unity. But everything is, is a being, is posited in being. Being reveals itself to our question

as the formal unity of the totality of all beings, as a *horizon of formal unity*.

(2) The question is an activity which posits the unity of being and knowing, which are identical in the unity of the act. The unity of the act exists when the question is asked, when it is posited in being. Because and insofar as the act is posited in being and as being, it is one: this one, self-identical being. Hence being is the ground of the unity of the existent, not only as a mere horizon of formal unity, but as *principle of real unity*.

(3) Insofar as something *is*, it is one, really identical with itself. Insofar as everything *is*, it is united with everything else. The fact that something *is* does not, by itself, distinguish it from anything. Being as being introduces no difference, no limit, no distinction. It posits pure identity and unity. Even as limited in different ways by their essence, finite beings keep this identity in their difference, as the formal identity of being in the real difference of beings.

The Inner Unity of Each Being

(1) Traditionally, a being is called one when it is undivided in itself and divided from all others. The former aspect refers to the inner unity of the being, the latter to its outer unity.

We can inquire only about that which we know that we can know. And we can know something only when it necessarily is itself. The self-identity of the object of the question is a condition of its possibility.

(2) From this self-identity follows the unity of each being. If the existent necessarily is itself, it is also necessarily *all* that which it is. In its identity all that which constitutes it is neces-

sarily posited. Otherwise, it would in part be itself and in part not, it would at the same time be itself and not be itself. Hence it is necessarily undivided in itself. It possesses what we may call the *identity of totality.*

(3) A being may have parts or no parts, may be composed or simple, divisible or indivisible. A simple being exists necessarily as one, in the pure identity of its totality. A composed being, although it has parts and is divisible, can be itself only when all these parts are given together. Only absolute being is absolutely simple. A finite being is composed of being and essence; these components are not necessarily united, so that such a being is contingent. However, if it is, the components must co-exist, the being is *one.*

Although unity is often expressed as a negative perfection in the sense of *not being divided,* it is in fact a positive perfection. It is the self-identity and self-presence of being with itself.

The Outer Unity of the Existent

(1) When we inquire or know about beings, we posit as a condition of the possibility of our question or knowledge, not only that each being is undivided in itself, but also that it is divided from all other beings, that it is not something different from what it is. This knowledge presupposes not only the knowledge of being as identity, but also that of being as difference. Only if there are finite beings which, on account of their essence, have realized different possibilities, can we speak of one and the other. For, as we have seen, finite beings are determined through their negative relation to others. Hence if there is a finite being, there must necessarily be more than one, at least two of them.

(2) As the being's necessary identity with itself made it *undivided in itself*, so its necessary non-identity with the other makes it *divided from all others*. The inner unity of a being consists in the fact that everything which it is, is posited. Its outer unity consists in the fact that nothing is posited in it which it is not. While the fact of being undivided in itself is not a merely negative perfection, the same cannot be said of being divided from all others. This is merely the negative differentiation of one being from all others. Here the positive element is the inner unity of the being by which it is identical with itself.

Unity and Multiplicity

If there are finite beings, there is necessarily at least the possibility of a multiplicity of them, since each individual being must be related to the others and be distinct from them in order to be fully determined. What is the relation between the multiplicity of beings and the unity of being?

(1) Every multiplicity presupposes unity. For there can be multiplicity only if every individual is itself one, distinct from the others, and constituting the multiplicity together with the others. Multiplicity presupposes the unity of each individual.

(2) Not only does it presuppose the unity of each individual, but also some unity in the multiplicity itself, that is, some unity in which the members agree. Multiplicity as such is possible only if in the multiplicity there is some unity. Without this unity there would only be disparate individuals, no real multiplicity. The members of the multiplicity must have at least something in common in order to be put together in the

123

same multiplicity. Being is this common feature of all the members of the multiplicity.

(3) Yet the multiplicity supposes also a diversity among its members. Otherwise, all of them would coincide and there would be no multiplicity. In the members of every multiplicity the common element is their being, the differentiating element, their essence. Underlying these two there must be a unity which no longer knows of a duality of being and essence, the identical unity of being and essence. This is being itself, whose essence is to be.

The Analogy of Unity

If unity is a transcendental property of being, if being is analogous, the unity of being too must be analogous. Every being is one, but in a different way. And inasmuch as it does not possess perfect unity, it refers beyond itself to pure and absolute unity.

(1) When a being is one among many, we may distinguish in it that through which it is itself and not the other from that through which it is one among many. We have here two aspects, which might eventually be separated. Hence, although every being is necessarily one, it may be more or less one, it may possess different degrees of inner unity, of undividedness, in itself. Such unity is not the pure unity of being, it is related to this higher unity of absolute being.

(2) When being is one among many, it is one in itself and also a part of a whole, it is taken up in a higher unity. This whole or higher unity itself may be part of a still higher unity, of a more comprehensive whole. Thus from the point of view

of its outer unity too, being may manifest different degrees of unity, which do not quite reach the unity of being itself. That is why our mind proceeds beyond these lower forms of unity, until it reaches a pure and perfect unity, which is no longer part of a higher whole, which is being itself and as a whole: the absolute unity as the totality and simplicity of absolute being.

(3) Thus unity passes from impure and imperfect forms to ever purer and more perfect forms. Such a passage is not brought about from outside. For every being is one, and every determination of being is itself a being, hence one. Therefore, the increasing determination of unity is, like that of being itself, an inner self-determination and self-realization of that which unity really is. Hence like being, unity is an analogous reality and like the concept of being, the concept of unity is not a univocal, but an analogous concept.

2. BEING AS TRUTH

The Question as Knowledge and Willing

When we know a being, we grasp it with our spirit. This supposes that this being is capable of being grasped by the spirit, that it possesses certain properties which make it fit for the spirit. When we grasp this being, these properties are unthematically co-known. We must now find out about them.

(1) Asking questions supposes that we wish to know, and that supposes that it is possible for us to know. The question reaches out towards that which may be known, which is known already to some extent, but not fully and exhaustively. We wish to know it further and that is why we inquire. Hence we can

125

ask questions only on the basis of knowledge. A first property of spiritual activity is *knowing*.

(2) But inquiring is not pure knowledge. We can no longer inquire when we know exhaustively. The question supposes a striving which goes beyond that which is already known towards more, which is not yet known, but knowable. Thus we discover a new aspect in our inquiring; beside knowing there is also *willing*. In the act of inquiring we posit the act of willing.

(3) In this way we have discovered *reductively*, in the act of inquiring, the duality of knowing and willing. To show that these two activities are the two necessary and also the two exclusive activities of the spirit can be done only *deductively*. For it is not enough to connect the duality of knowing and willing with that of truth and goodness, since the latter duality can be established only by pointing to the spiritual activities of knowing and willing.

Spiritual Activity as Knowing and Willing

(1) We have shown that the act of inquiring and of knowing supposes a distinction of subject and object and an identity of both of them. Since the identity of the act does not suppress, but presupposes the difference of subject and object, it may be posited in the subject or in the object.

(2) If the act is posited in the subject, it is a self-actuation of the subject in its object, insofar as the latter is posited in the subject. But when the object is thus posited in the subject, it enters into the identity of being and knowing, it is posited in the self-luminosity of the subject, as an object of which the subject is aware. This self-actuation of the finite spirit in that

126

which is other than itself, insofar as the other is posited not in itself, but in the spirit, is called *knowing*. It is an activity whereby the subject posits in itself as known that which is not itself, without suppressing its otherness, but rather presupposing it and thus knowing the other as other.

(3) The act through which subject and object are identified may also be posited in the object. In this case, it is a self-actuation of the subject in its object, insofar as the latter exists in itself. The subject steps outside of itself, as it were, and gives itself to the other. It affirms the other as the other is in itself and strives towards it in its otherness. This is precisely what we call *to will*. It is an activity in which the subject actuates itself in the direction of the other as object of its volition, trying to suppress the difference between subject and object and positing itself in the other.

Ontic Truth and Logical Truth

(1) We may inquire about everything which *is*. But we can inquire only about what we know already to some extent and about which we know that we may know more. For inquiring presupposes the possibility of knowing and knowledge of this possibility. Hence inquiring presupposes that the object of the inquiry may be known. Since we may inquire about everything, this presupposes that absolutely everything is knowable. It is a condition of the possibility of our inquiring that we should know everything as knowable. Hence all beings are knowable and pre-known as such. But that which is knowable is *true*. Hence every being is true.

(2) Because and insofar as it *is*, each and every being may be the object of an act of knowledge. It is within the reach of

the spirit, fit to enter into it. It is intelligible. We call this intelligibility *truth,* but only in a first and basic sense, that of *ontic truth.* This is the truth of the beings which goes together with their being. It implies the possibility, not the actuality, of the knowledge of these objects. Of itself being is such that it may be known.

When there is actual knowledge, when the object in the act of knowing corresponds to the object as it exists in itself, we speak of true knowledge in the sense of *logical truth.* This is the truth of knowledge as it corresponds to being.

Ontic truth consists in the fact that the being itself is fit to be known. Logical truth consists in the fact that the act of knowledge fits the object, corresponds to it, knows it as it is. Traditionally, truth has been defined as the correspondence between or the adequation of knowledge and being. Such correspondence may take place in two directions. Either knowledge corresponds to or agrees with pre-existing being, in which case there is logical truth; or being corresponds to or agrees with knowledge, stands open for it, is within its reach, in which case there is ontic truth.

(3) This differentiation tells us about the relation between ontic and logical truth. On the one hand, from the point of view of the act of knowledge, ontic truth, as the possibility of being known, is only a potentiality; it is transformed into actuality by the act of knowledge, thus becoming logical truth. On the other hand, from the formal point of view, the roles are reversed: it is possible for the spirit to know all beings. This possibility derives from the fact that all beings are ontically true.

(4) No being lies wholly beyond the reach of the spirit, not even of the finite spirit. Yet the latter can never know all

that which is thus knowable for it. The finite spirit stands open for unlimited knowledge, for the infinite horizon of being as knowable. On the other hand, as finite, it can only know a finite range of it. Hence the ceaseless dynamism and dialectic of the spirit which, beyond that which it happens to know, reaches out for more being to be known.

Ontological Truth

Beings as beings are related to the spirit. Spirit as spirit is related to all beings. In order to discover the foundation of this relation, we must proceed beyond ontic and logical to ontological truth.

(1) Beings are the object, the spirit is the subject. But this duality must be based upon an underlying unity. The fact that being and spirit are related must be explained. If there were nothing in common between them, we would not see how all beings are knowable and how the spirit can know all of them.

(2) The underlying unity is being. Both the object and the subject *are*. We know that being means an identification of knowing and being. Basically, being is self-knowledge and knowledge is the self-presence of being. This identity of being and knowing as the ultimate ground of ontic and logical truth is *ontological truth*. It is the truth not merely of beings and of our knowledge of them, but of beings as knowing themselves and known by themselves, in one identical act.

(3) Heidegger rejects the traditional interpretation of truth as a correspondence between mind and thing. He wishes to return to the original sense of the Greek word for truth, *alètheia,*

which means unconcealedness, the fact of not being hidden or concealed, of being open or manifest. He claims that traditional metaphysics explains truth by means of the spirit who possesses it, but that it does not explain the spirit itself. It is a metaphysics of subjectivity, which ignores the basic reality of being.

However, Heidegger overlooks the fact that traditional philosophy knew, besides logical truth as correspondence between mind and being, an ontic truth which corresponds somewhat to his *unconcealedness* of being. Moreover, both ontic and logical truth are based upon ontological truth, so that the duality object-subject must be interpreted in the light of being itself. Being, in its purity, is self-conscious self-presence in the identity of knowing and being. The subject is that in which being reaches self-awareness. The object is that which reaches self-awareness in the spiritual activity of the subject.

(4) In this sense, Idealism is correct when it claims that basically all being is spirit: spiritual being, spiritual self-actuation in self-presence. It is only in the conscious activity of the spirit that non-spiritual beings come entirely into their own. However, Idealism is wrong when it denies that the knowing activity of the finite spirit presupposes beings in their ontic truth. Idealism ignores the analogy of being and admits the univocity of spiritual being.

(5) Some beings are so limited in their being that they cannot perform spiritual activities. But pure being is spirit, and the more a being is, the more spiritual its activity. Hence there is not a static equivalence between being and spirit, but there is a dynamic identity between the two of them. A being which is too limited to reach spiritual self-actuation, strives to overcome this limit and to reach this self-actuation, at least by offering itself, through its ontic truth, to the spirit, so that the latter may grant it the actuation it cannot achieve by itself.

Infinite Truth

(1) Within finite reality truth assumes the two forms of ontic and of logical truth. The finite being is knowable by the spirit, the finite spirit knows about being. This duality presupposes an underlying unity which we have called ontological truth. But in finite actuation ontological truth, as identity of knowledge and being, is always only given as a *relative unity*. Hence it cannot be the ultimate ground of unity we are looking for. The finite spirit is not the ground of ontic truth, nor is finite being the origin of the spirit. Thus the mutual relation between that which is knowable and that which knows presupposes a higher condition of their possibility. The relative unity of knowing and being presupposes an *absolute unity*.

(2) This absolute unity is found in absolute being, which coincides perfectly with itself in the luminous self-identity of knowledge and self-consciousness. In it, subject and object, logical and ontic truth, are fully identified.

The Analogy of Truth

Since truth is a transcendental property of being and being is analogous, the truth of being too must be analogous. This is evident from the following considerations.

(1) Every being is knowable, it is ontically true. But if it cannot become aware of its own truth, this truth is only a potential truth, which only an act of the intellect may transform into logical truth. But even this truth is imperfect, with its opposition of subject and object, and supposes an underlying ontological truth as the actuation of the identity of being and know-

131

ing. Finally, ontological truth itself is only a relative unity of being and knowing, unless it embraces the whole of being in unlimited self-awareness, in infinite truth.

(2) Hence the truth of being is, as it were, driven from finite and imperfect forms of truth to its primordial and pure form as it exists in the self-actuation of absolute being. The lower forms of truth are not suppressed by the higher ones, but absorbed and transcended by them, and brought to their full realization. Hence, like being and unity, truth is *analogous,* and like the concepts of being and of unity, the concept of truth is an analogous concept.

3. BEING AS GOODNESS

From Knowing to Willing

The finite spirit actuates itself in the identity of subject and object. When this actuation is posited in the subject, so that the object is taken up into it, we have an act of knowledge. When the actuation is posited in the object, so that the subject is drawn towards it, we have an act of willing.

(1) In knowledge, the object is grasped as the other. Yet this other is grasped as such only insofar as it has entered the subject. It is not grasped in itself, in its real exteriority to the subject. Knowledge identifies subject and object intentionally, not really. A deeper kind of identity is possible, in which the identification is real, in which the subject is united to the object not as it is in the subject, but as it is in itself.

The object in itself is really different from the subject in itself. This difference is not suppressed by the act of willing. As long as it continues to exist, the identity which is essential

132

to being is imperfect. It remains an intended, not a fully achieved identity of the subject with its object. The subject does not really actuate itself *in* the object, but towards it, as it remains opposed to the subject as something other. However, in its actuation the subject transcends itself, in order to identify itself with the object. It posits the other as other, it wills it for its own sake, because and insofar as it is the other. By doing so, it posits the other unconditionally. Hence to will means to posit unconditionally, to assert the other unconditionally, because and insofar as it is or should be. Willing is the unconditional self-positing of the spirit in the direction of the other, in a striving for the suppression of the difference with the other, by means of a real identification with it.

(2) We see, then, that the basic constituent of volition is the unconditioned positing and affirming of the other for its own sake, which is nothing else but *love*. Thus originally and properly, to will is not to try to grasp or to possess the other, in order to reach for oneself a higher degree of ontological perfection. In its primordial purity, willing rather is willing the other not for our own sake, but for its sake. It is an unconditional affirmation and valorization of the other and at the same time a self-actuation aimed at the other as a self-donation to it. Willing turns into a striving to possess the other only when it refers to objects of a lower kind. Since such objects possess no ultimate value in themselves, since they are made for the spirit, the spirit cannot reach its actuation by giving itself to them. It can actuate itself and the object only by referring the latter to itself.

(3) Like knowledge, willing can extend to all that which is, to everything. In a certain sense, it extends even further than knowing, for the latter reaches beings only as they are posited in the subject, as the object of its act, whereas willing and love reach the object in itself.

133

Ontic and Actuated Goodness

(1) Inquiring is not only an act of knowledge, but also an act of the will, because we wish to know, because we strive towards more knowledge. This supposes that the object of our inquiry can be desired and willed. We can inquire about everything, hence everything can be desired and willed. We can inquire only when we know already about the object of our inquiry, not only as something which can be known but also as something about which more knowledge is desirable. Hence all beings as such are desirable, at least in the sense that more knowledge may be desired about them. Therefore, in this sense, all beings are objects of our will and are known as such. But to be the object of our will is to be *good*. Therefore, insofar as it is, every being is good.

Furthermore, like knowing, willing is a spiritual activity of being as being. Since every being as such is a possible object of such spiritual activity, since therefore every being as such is an object of the will, every being as such is good.

Finally, willing, as a spiritual and conscious act, follows upon knowing as a spiritual activity. We can only will that which we know. But we can will all that which we can know. And since we can know absolutely everything, we can also will everything. Every being, as such, is a possible object of the will, is good.

(2) All of this shows that being as such is a possible object of my striving or willing. But since, as we showed above, willing, in its pure and original form, is a welcoming of the other and a self-donation to it, the fact that every being is a possible object of the will means that it is a possible object of love, that it is *lovable*. Hence every being, by the very fact that it is, is a possible and worthy object of a loving affirmation and of the will's self-donation. This is *goodness,* but only in a first and

provisional sense of *ontic goodness,* of goodness which goes together with the very being of each existent. It implies only the possibility, not the reality, of actual willing or loving.

When such actual willing or loving is present, the being is actuated in the goodness which belongs to it. Then ontic goodness becomes *actuated goodness,* just as the act of knowledge transforms ontic truth into logical (actuated) truth. But since the act of knowing posits the object in the subject, while the act of willing reaches the object in itself, actuated goodness is posited in the object itself. It is the object's ontic goodness, insofar as it is actuated in itself, insofar as it is the actual object of the will.

(3) The doctrine of the ontic goodness of being stands mid-way between two positions which might be called the *rationalism of values* and the *irrationalism of values.* The former totally identifies being and goodness, or being and value. Goodness no longer adds anything to being. Spinoza is the most famous representative of this doctrine.

On the other hand, irrationalism of values separates being and value completely. Being as such is considered as lacking all value, the latter is a determination which differs from being, which cannot be known, but only *felt.* Max Scheler is one of the best known spokesmen of this position.

(4) Therefore, it may be worth while to explain the relation which exists between value and being. (*a*) The good concretely means being insofar as it possesses goodness or value. Value, on the other hand, means abstractly or formally the goodness which belongs to something. (*b*) Ontic goodness means that a reality deserves to be desired, willed, loved, without implying that a determined subject actually desires or loves it. Value, on the other hand, implies a reference to a subject, it is always a *value*

135

for somebody. The ontic goodness of a being does not mean that it is actually desirable for or desired by every being. That depends on the structure or the finality of each being. The philosophy of values considers mainly the finality, especially the moral perfectibility, of the human subject. (*c*) The philosophy of values claims that values *are* not. They belong to a domain of objectively valid, yet not real, but ideal axiological qualities, which are felt by axiological feeling and realized by axiological activity. The great difficulty against this assertion is that it supposes a realm of entities which would be transcendent to being.

In the philosophy of values, the grasping of the values is generally attributed to some kind of *value feeling* or *axiological feeling.* This feeling is an activity which differs from knowing and willing, and constitutes a third essential spiritual activity. Yet this kind of feeling seems to consist of a mixture of immediate, quasi-intuitive knowledge and some vaguely felt, implicit reactions of the will. It is a total reaction of the whole person in his bodily-spiritual unity. It implies an immediate spiritual insight, not an irrational emotional reaction. On the other hand, since it refers to an insight into values, it is a knowledge which implies also an active attitude of the whole person, which appeals to the totality of his personality, which makes him react as a whole; this may produce the impression that it consists merely or exclusively of feeling.

All of this allows us to point out a middle position between axiological rationalism and irrationalism. On the one hand, each being as being is good, and this goodness is rooted in its being. On the other hand, when we grasp a being as being, we have not yet grasped it as good or valuable. This implies a relation to our will. Being is good insofar as it possesses a relation to our will. Being and the good are really (materially) identical, they are conceptually (formally) different.

Ontological Goodness

(1) Every being is ontically good, and the finite spirit is capable of transforming each being's ontic goodness into actuated goodness. On this level of ontic and actuated goodness, that which deserves to be willed or loved stands opposed to that which can will or love, as object to subject. Underlying this opposition there must be a unifying foundation, which explains how the two terms are not only opposed to each other but also designed for each other.

(2) The underlying foundation is being. Both the object and the subject of willing *are*. The object is each being in its own ontic goodness. Since being always actuates itself, the object of willing, as being, also actuates itself, it turns into something which is *good for itself*. As such, it may further become the term of the striving of some other being, thus turning into something which is *good for some other*. It follows that the object of the axiological relation—the ontic good—is also always its subject, as it actuates itself in its own value, thus positing an original *identity of being and striving*, that is, the identity of being as value and being as actuation of value, the identity in being of the subject and the object of the axiological relation.

Something similar happens in the subject of the striving. It strives towards an increase of its own perfection, thus actuating its own nature as a value which is not only to be maintained but also to be increased. In order to increase itself, it strives towards some other being, the object of the striving, thus actuating this object. It follows that the subject, too, of the axiological relation, the existent which strives after some value, is always also the object of this relation, since it actuates itself in its own value. Once more we have here an *identity of being and striving*, that is, an identity of being as that which deserves to be willed and of being as that which actuates the value, an identity in being of the subject and the object of the axiological relation.

(3) As long as the self-actuation does not reach being as being (in the non-spiritual existents), the striving is not conscious, the subject is not aware of it. And the values which such a striving intends are still relative values, comprised in a restricted horizon of values. A striving for the good within the unconditional horizon of value occurs only when we arrive at the *self-actuation of the spirit,* in which the striving becomes conscious. The spirit actuates itself in the horizon of being, thus transcending its own limits towards the unlimited totality of being. This reaching beyond its own limits for the unlimited being is really a striving, a willing. Hence the self-actuation of the spirit is essentially a volition. The finite spirit strives towards the totality of being insofar as it posits and asserts itself in its own perfection, the perfection which it possesses already and which is still to be realized. Thus spiritual self-actuation is essentially a self-volition of the spirit. Here too we have a primordial *identity of being and willing.* Being is willing and willing is being.

Hence, as we have seen above that being basically is the same as knowing (ontological truth), we see here that being basically is the same as willing. This is *ontological goodness,* the basis which unifies ontic and actuated goodness. Ontological goodness is not the object of the striving of some other being, it is the goodness of being itself in itself, as it wills and loves itself and is willed and loved by itself.

(4) Spirit means, on the one hand, the active identification of being and knowing, and on the other hand, the active identification of being and willing; consequently, it is also the active identification of knowing and willing. This identification comes before the differentiation of knowing and willing. For

every spiritual being is essentially knowing and willing in perfect unity. Insofar as the spirit is spirit, it is self-luminous, a conscious, self-aware actuation. Insofar as the spirit is actuation, it actuates and fulfills itself by willing itself.

Yet the self-actuation of the finite spirit also implies the difference between knowing and willing. For, as finite, the spirit can actuate itself only by actuating the other. This brings about the distinction of subject and object. But we have seen that this distinction entails a distinction between knowing and willing, according to whether the actuation is posited in the subject (knowing) or in the object (willing).

This basic knowing and willing—as the self-knowledge and the self-volition of the spirit—is not a separate act, which would precede each conscious act of knowing and willing. Neither does it coincide with the very being of the spirit. It is rather an activity which is unthematically co-performed in every act of the spirit, whether it be an act of knowledge or an act of volition.

Infinite Goodness

(1) Like ontological truth, ontological goodness remains forever finite in the self-actuation of the finite spirit. Being as a whole stands infinitely above the finite spirit and its actuation, it can never be reached by it. That is why the finite unity of being and willing cannot be the ultimate foundation of the relation of value. It presupposes an *infinite unity* of being and willing.

(2) Absolute being is the original unlimited fullness and unity of all perfections. But willing is a pure perfection, so that it is posited in all its purity and in unlimited fullness in absolute being. Absolute being is therefore infinite loving, infinite willing, which actuates to its fullest possible extent all possi-

bilities of loving and willing. It follows that whatever in being is worthy of being willed and loved is perfectly assimilated in its self-actuation. Absolute being is absolute willing and absolute loving, it is infinite will and infinite love.

(3) We can now understand why every being is ontically good. For every being is posited into being by absolute being, its first cause. The absolute activity of this first cause derives from its absolute will and love. It follows that every being, insofar as it is, is also willed and loved by absolute being. It must therefore be worthy of being willed and loved, that is, it must be ontically good.

(4) An objection might be raised against the statement that goodness is a pure perfection. Goodness, so goes the objection, supposes some striving; but striving supposes imperfection and limitation, since that which is perfect and unlimited can never be conceived as striving towards more.

The objection carries for all finite striving. Finite striving is essentially a reaching out and a *grasping of values,* which the finite subject needs in order to achieve its own fulfilment. But there is also a striving which is rather a *welcoming of value,* an acquiescing in it, an opening up for it, an enjoyment of it. This kind of striving is already present to some extent in the highest kinds of finite striving, as they crave the intellectual value of truth, the aesthetic value of beauty, the ethical value of virtue, but especially the personal value of love. Yet, in finite beings this acquiescing, welcoming striving is never present in full purity, it is always accompanied by and blended with some reaching out or grasping kind of striving.

The former kind of striving is obviously not a pure perfection, since it essentially implies some limitation. But the latter kind, which consists in a pure welcoming, donation, and enjoying, implies no limitation and should therefore be considered as a pure perfection.

(5) Every being as being is good. Goodness is a transcendental determination of being as such. Since being is analogous, the goodness of being too is analogous. This fact may be shown by reflecting upon what has been said about goodness heretofore. All beings possess ontic goodness, each one according to its degree of being. Ontic goodness turns into actuated goodness when it actually becomes the object of some striving. Underlying both, so we have established, is ontological goodness, which reaches its unlimited peak in absolute goodness, as it exists in absolute being. In all of its manifestations, goodness really exists; thus the word is not used equivocally. Yet it exists in different degrees; thus the word is not used univocally. Hence the term *goodness* is used analogously, and goodness, as it is displayed throughout the realm of reality, is analogous.

The Problem of Evil

If the goodness of being is analogous, there must be in the beings many instances of limited goodness. Should we not say also that over and above such limitations of goodness, there are cases of total absence of it, in which being is not good at all, but simply evil or bad? This supposition raises one of the most debated problems in the history of human thinking, that of the nature of evil.

(1) The question about the nature of evil has received a few radical answers, in the sense of absolute optimism and absolute pessimism. The former claims that everything is good, nothing is evil. The latter asserts that everything is evil, nothing is good. Optimism lies in the line of rationalistic and pantheistic

thinking. Thus when Spinoza interpreted everything as finite modifications, or as self-determinations of the one divine substance, deriving from it with inner and absolute necessity, there was for him no room for any evil. Another instance is the optimism of Leibniz, for whom the world was the best of all possible worlds. Hegel claimed that every finite reality possesses its metaphysically necessary place within the dialectical self-development of the Absolute; hence for him evil too has to be, although as a moment of the process which should be "sublated" (*aufgehoben*). Pessimism, on the other hand, is most typically represented by Arthur Schopenhauer, who explained the world as the product of a blind, senseless drive; whatever exists, derives from evil: the world is the worst possible world.

More frequent than these extreme positions are the intermediate ones, which admit the reality both of good and of evil, but which attribute different importance to both. On the one hand, there is dualism, which teaches the positive nature of the good and of evil, and claims that there exist two ultimate principles of reality, independent of each other: a principle of good and a principle of evil. This doctrine seems to have originated in Parsiism, it continued to live in Gnosticism and in Manicheism, and it was revived more recently by Jakob Böhme. The latter ultimately reduced both of them, the principle of light and the principle of darkness, to the unity of God, although in his version each one acts on its own and fights the other in the world. Along the same line, Schelling, in his theosophic period, interpreted the duality of the principle of the ideal and of the principle of the real as principles of light and of darkness. With him, too, this duality is rooted in the unity of the Absolute. In the Absolute, the dark principle of reality ("nature in God") is dominated by the luminous principle of ideality, and in this way it is not evil, while in the world it escapes this harmonious subordination and turns into the principle of evil. In this way, the dualism has for a great part disappeared: evil no longer derives from a substantially evil principle, it comes from a negative element, the lack of order and harmony. Thus Schelling came near to the classic doctrine of Christian philosophy, although he explicitly rejected it. For, according to the patristic-Scholastic doctrine, which Augustine developed in opposition to Gnosticism and Manicheism, and which was taken over by the whole Scholastic tradition, evil does not consist in a positive, but in a negative element, in a lack of being, which causes the absence of a perfection required by a being. This teaching may be explained as follows.

(2) Evil in the widest sense, whether physical evil (pain and suffering) or moral evil (sin), consists either in something positive or in something negative. But all that which is positive, is being, and we have shown that being as being is good. Hence evil cannot consist in something positive, but only in something negative, in a negation of being. In this case, it must consist either in a total negation of being, which suppresses being as such, or in a partial negation, which lets being subsist but denies something in it. If evil consists in a total negation, it takes away all being and it is nothing; there is no more evil. Hence the negation can only be partial: without taking away being itself, it takes away a certain perfection of it.

This perfection which is taken away cannot be a substantial property which belongs to the very being of the existent; otherwise, evil would simply make of this being some other being, it would transform A into B. It would no longer be evil, but a substantial transformation. Hence the perfection which is taken away by evil can only be an accidental perfection, one which does not constitute the being as such. Even here the accidental perfection cannot be one which is absolutely required for the subsistence of the being in question, else we would have the same result as above. Thus the only perfection which evil may take away in a being is an accidental perfection which the being

143

should possess, although its absence does not destroy the being's nature. Such are the perfections which a being should develop in order to be really itself, perfections which are required by the being's own finality. When they are absent, the being lacks something which it should possess. Evil consists in such a lack. Hence evil is not something positive, but something negative: it is the non-existence of an accidental perfection which the being's own nature and finality demands.

Beauty as the Unity of the Transcendentals

The unity of the transcendentals, as unity of the true and the good, results in *beauty*, which is one more transcendental property of being, although it occupies a peculiar position among them.

(1) Aquinas defined the beautiful as that which, when contemplated or apprehended, produces enjoyment. This definition distinguishes two aspects in beauty which show that it is related to the true and to the good. The beautiful is *good*, it attracts us, we look for it. But it differs from other forms of goodness because it is something which we wish to look at, to contemplate, something whose aspect we wish to enjoy. This element connects the beautiful with the *true*, since it involves an element of knowledge. Of course, not every act of knowledge results into beauty, but only intuitive and contemplative knowledge, which allows the object to work upon and to charm the subject; beauty does not derive from rational thinking but from immediate intuition. In such an intuition our drive for beauty finds satisfaction.

(2) The question can therefore be asked whether beauty is restricted to the domain of the senses. For the only kind of intuition we possess is sense intuition. It is a fact that in its

144

first and original sense beauty supposes some sense intuition: we enjoy beauty in a work of art or in a spectacle of nature. But what then of the beauty of truth, of virtue, of God? Is the term used only metaphorically in these expressions?

On this problem opinions are divided. German Idealism, especially that of Schelling and Hegel, claimed that the beautiful is the embodiment or reflection of spiritual realities in the domain of the senses. They admit no real spiritual beauty, they deny the transcendental nature of beauty.

(3) Yet it is a fact that even when we grasp certain supra-sensible contents, we may experience a feeling of beauty. Such is the case for some metaphysical or religious truths, not those which are reached through reasoning and concepts, but those which are known in intuitive immediacy. The same is true for moral goodness, virtue, sanctity, and especially for the infinite greatness, wisdom, and goodness of God, which, although beyond the reach of the senses, may produce a feeling of beauty in those who approach them by some kind of spiritual contemplation.

(4) The difficulty remains, however, that we have no real spiritual or intellectual intuition, that we possess only sense intuition. We may overcome this difficulty by pointing out that our sense intuition is always penetrated or animated by intellectual or spiritual knowledge. Beauty is not accessible to mere sense knowledge, it appeals to the spirit, although through the agency of the senses. Hence we should not separate the two levels of knowledge which philosophy distinguishes in us. Our first contact with reality always implies both the senses and the intellect. Even after we have considered the intellectual element separately through abstraction, we should put it back into its sense context and thus enrich our way of approaching reality.

145

It is not when the intellect abstractly considers its proper share in our knowledge that we meet with beauty; only in the first naïve total contact or in the later similar contact, enriched by reflection, may we enjoy the spectacle of beauty. It is the spirit in us who enjoys this spectacle, although the spirit in conjunction with the senses.

(5) What is the specific content of beauty as contrasted with truth and goodness? It seems that the essence of beauty consists precisely in a combination of truth and goodness. The beautiful is the true, insofar as it satisfies our striving; it is the good, insofar as it satisfies a desire for knowledge, which comes to rest in its contemplation. Hence the beautiful is the true insofar as it coincides with the good; it is the good insofar as it coincides with the true. In this sense, beauty is the specific result of the unity of the transcendentals: the unity of truth and goodness is beauty.

4. FREEDOM AND POSSIBILITY[1]

Freedom of the Will

(1) All beings must act. The finite spirit must actuate itself through action. As a spirit it does so, through knowledge and volition, in the horizon of being, hence it continually reaches out for the unlimited totality of being. Since as a finite spirit it cannot embrace this unlimited totality, it has to reach for other finite beings. It has to assimilate others, but since it acts in the horizon of being it is not forced to assimilate any determined being. None of them comes up to its unlimited horizon. Nor

[1] Although freedom and possibility are not transcendentals, they are treated here because they presuppose many of the notions which we have explained in the preceding pages.

146

does the spirit's own nature force it to choose this rather than that. Its nature forces it to assimilate, but not to assimilate this or that being. Hence the finite spirit must necessarily determine itself to assimilate this or that being. But the self-determination of an activity by the agent itself is *freedom*. Hence the finite spirit necessarily acts freely.

(2) Thus we have established freedom *deductively*. We might also do it *reductively*, through a phenomenological analysis of human activity. In our entire human activity, freedom and awareness of it are presupposed. Even if we deny it theoretically, we cannot abstain from acting as if we were free. We have to choose, to decide between possible courses of action. We appeal to the freedom of others through advice and exhortation; social life is full of relations which suppose freedom. Notions such as good and evil, justice and injustice, virtue and vice, do not make sense without freedom. The awareness of our freedom is an unthematic, lived, or exercised kind of knowledge which accompanies all of our activity.

(3) In freedom we discover the original unity of knowing and willing. Every spiritual activity supposes some self-awareness and self-volition, although both may be unthematic. When the spiritual activity turns towards the other, knowledge and willing become distinct activities. Yet they continue to refer intimately to each other, and to determine each other. All knowledge is, as activity, determined by some volition. And all volition is, as spiritual and conscious, determined by some knowledge. The volition which is a constitutive element of the act of knowing is no longer a volition as contrasted with knowledge, it is absorbed in the knowledge as *its exercise*. And the knowledge which is a constitutive element of volition is no longer a knowledge as contrasted with volition, it is absorbed in the volition as *its specification*.

Possibility

Spiritual activity is free. This or that action may be performed, but it does not have to be performed. It is not necessary, but possible. Hence freedom supposes possibility; possibility is a condition of freedom.

(1) Possible is that which may be. Possibility is the fact that something may be. The possibility of the possible supposes that there exists something which, as a cause, has the power of putting into being some other thing as its effect. This is *external* possibility: something may come into being insofar as it may be posited by some other being as by its cause. This presupposes, however, that its nature or essence allows it to be put into being. External possibility presupposes *internal* possibility: something may exist insofar as its own essence permits.

(2) Internal possibility is present whenever the essence of a being does not contain contradictory or incompatible notes or determinations. Otherwise, the being would be and not be simultaneously this or that. Inner possibility supposes the compatibility of a being's inner determinations or notes, the absence of contradiction in its definition.

(3) Compatibility supposes several determinations. Each one of them too must be possible. Each may be further composed of more determinations, to which the same rule applies. We cannot go on indefinitely and must therefore arrive at an original ground of the possibility, which comes before any compatibility and is the foundation of the possibility of every simple being or of the ultimate simple determinations of each being. This ultimate ground is being itself. Should being not be, nothing would be even innerly possible, there would be no norm for the possibility or impossibility of beings.

The same can be shown by examining the notion of incompatibility. This presupposes the principle of contradiction or of identity: Being is, insofar as it is, necessarily itself. Hence all contradictions must be excluded. But the ontic principle of identity is based on the ontological principle of identity: Being necessarily is being, it necessarily excludes non-being. Hence inner possibility is ultimately based on the necessity of being.

It follows that reality is previous to possibility. Only because being is are things possible. Without being there would be no compatibility or incompatibility of determinations, there would be no principle of identity, nothing would be possible.

(4) Although inner possibility is an absolute prerequisite for the existence of any being, which even absolute being cannot change or ignore, this does not mean that absolute being is, as it were, ruled from without by this condition. On the contrary, this condition itself derives from absolute being. The principle of identity, which underlies the requirement of compatibility, is ultimately the absolute necessity of being to be itself. Absolute being cannot will not to be itself; neither can it will that the contradictory or impossible should be.

The Absolute as Ground of all Possibility

(1) Beings are composed of being and essence. A being is possible when its essence can be put into being. Yet the ultimate norm cannot lie in the being's essence, since the latter does not exist before the being itself; it only co-exists with and in the existing being. Hence the ultimate ground must lie in being; not, however, in the being of this particular existent, since this being too is an inner constituent of the existent, posited only with and in it; nor in the being of other existents, since they too are contingent and for them too the question of the ground

149

of their possibility arises. Hence we must go back again to being itself, insofar as it is prior to the being of all finite, real, and possible existents. Only absolute being can supply the norm which decides whether and how finite being is possible. The ultimate ground of the possibility of finite beings is absolute being.

(2) How does absolute being constitute the ground of the possibility of finite beings? Finite beings are constituted of being and limiting essence. Hence our question becomes: (*a*) How is being possible in finite beings? (*b*) How is their limiting essence possible?

(*a*) The pure perfection of being in the finite existent is made possible by absolute being. All pure perfections of being, which are found in the finite existent, pre-exist really and necessarily, although analogously, and in an infinitely more perfect way ("eminently") in absolute being. They are possible in the finite existent because and insofar as they pre-exist in absolute being.

(*b*) Finite beings pre-exist "eminently" in absolute being, insofar as they are constituted by pure perfections. They do not pre-exist in it in this way insofar as their being is limited. This limitation does not pre-exist as such in absolute being. But it is pre-known by it, it pre-exists intentionally in its knowledge. The finite being does not pre-exist in absolute being as an object, but rather as a *project*. It is projected by the knowledge of absolute being and thus posited in its possibility. Since absolute being is perfectly self-conscious, it knows, not objectively, but projectively, all possible ways and forms in which finite beings may share being.

(3) The relation which we have explained between absolute being and the possibility of the finite existent illustrates the *exemplary causality* of the model upon the reproduction. An

exemplary cause is something which may be imitated by another existent, something which, through its imitable essence, exerts a certain influence upon another. Insofar as it exerts such an influence, it is a real cause. Yet, like the final cause, it supposes an efficient cause to become active. While the final cause acts immediately upon the will, the exemplary cause acts immediately upon the intellect, which knows the model and induces the will to reproduce it. The exemplary cause is related to the formal cause, since it provides the mind with the form which is to be reproduced in the object. But unlike the formal cause it does not enter into the object as its constituent element. It is an external cause.

Infinite Freedom

(1) If the possible is to become real, it must be realized by a cause. A cause which can produce being as being can produce absolutely all possible beings. The totality of all possible beings is unlimited, since no limited sum of finite beings can exhaust the infinite possibilities of being. Only the unlimited being can produce an unlimited amount of beings. It follows that the finite being is transferred from possibility to actuality by the infinite will, by absolute being.

(2) As infinite knowledge and infinite willing, infinite being knows all the knowable and loves all the good. This does not mean that all possible beings are necessarily realized by absolute will. All possibilities cannot be realized simultaneously, because the realization of one excludes that of another. In its infinite willing, absolute being necessarily decides freely what beings will be realized and what beings will not be realized. But a volition which decides between possible realizations is called *free*. Hence the act through which finite beings are transferred

from possibility to reality proceeds from the freedom of infinite will, from infinite freedom.

(3) Finite beings, even spiritual beings, cannot produce a being as being, although they know and will being in the absolute horizon of being. The reason is that finite activity does not posit being but presupposes it. It does not posit the substantial reality but only accidental realities of its object. It does not make but modify them. All of this helps us to understand the notion of *creation,* the production of beings out of nothing. Finite beings produce something out of something, their activity presupposes a subject which may receive it. Infinite being creates, produces something out of nothing, without presupposing any subject which might receive its activity.

VI.

BEING IN THE WORLD

WE have started from the question. From it we have derived
the fact that finite being is composed of being, essence, and
activity. In the question, too, we have discovered the transcendental properties of being: unity, truth, and goodness. But as
long as we consider the question only as a spiritual activity, we
have not fully understood it. Should the inquirer be pure spirit,
he would be unable to inquire as we do, about other things
which appear to us, and about ourself to whom these things
appear. Therefore, we must now inquire explicitly about the
question as an activity in the world. Thus we shall discover that
the inquirer is not pure spirit, but spirit in matter, subsisting
in a *material* world. This will help us understand the nature
of matter, of materiality as such, and the nature of the material
things in the world. But we live not only in a material world,
but also, and essentially, in a *personal* world, always already
involved in some social group, with other persons. This knowledge will help us to establish the basic structures of the person
in the world.

1. THE MATERIAL WORLD

Inquiring and Awareness of the Other

We can and we must ask questions. As a rule, they refer to
nearby realities: What is this? What is that? This is the starting

153

point of all inquiring, and only from thence may we inquire beyond all particular beings about being as such.

(1) When we inquire, *What is this?*, we know the answer already to some extent, since we speak of *this*. But we know also that there is more to know, we inquire about it by asking *what* it is. *This* is the thing about which we inquire, *what* is the object of the inquiry, pre-known to some extent but not yet fully known. The question as question is possible only because an object is presented to us about which we inquire. This object is given to us without intermediaries, directly. We know it and we do not know it. We know it, otherwise we would be unable to inquire about it; we do not know it, otherwise we would not have to inquire about it. It follows that this object is not a product of our own mind, that it is not set in being by us, otherwise we would know all about it. This knowledge is *receptive,* not productive knowledge. The question presupposes receptive knowledge.

(2) When we inquire about the other, our question presupposes the conditions of its possibility. We may inquire about them and try to find out what we are, what makes us capable of and obliged to ask questions. Inquiring about ourself presupposes that we know about ourself to some extent, that we are aware of ourself. It presupposes also that we do not know everything about ourself. Hence we are present to ourself in knowledge, and absent from ourself, because we do not know. Most of the time we are not self-present, but outside of ourself with the other. From the other we can return to ourself in reflection. Our knowledge starts with the other; thematically, we know the other first, ourself only in a second stage, through reflection.

(3) Thus we are not pure spirit. A pure spirit must always be aware of itself, knowing about itself. For every being necessarily acts, and the activity of spirit is spiritual knowledge, which

implies luminous self-awareness. Hence the pure spirit's first object is itself. If man knows about others first, about himself only afterwards, he is not pure spirit. There is in him a non-spiritual principle, which is called *materiality,* and which may be defined as the inner ground in a being's essence which explains why this being is not present to itself, but outside of itself with the other.

Therefore, we have reductively established man's materiality, starting from the receptive nature of his knowledge. Next we shall show deductively that receptive knowledge of a finite spirit supposes materiality, that it is essentially sense knowledge.

Receptivity and Materiality

(1) Every finite spirit necessarily has a horizon of otherness. Only by opposing itself to the other can it know itself. The other is not absolute being, it is a restricted domain of finite beings, it is the projected horizon of its world. This projected horizon involves no actual knowledge yet, but only the possibility of knowledge. It becomes actual only when other beings are known within this horizon.

This actual knowledge is receptive, the other is given as its object. That means that, although it is presented to the subject, it remains different from it. It gives itself to the subject, not in its substantial being, but through some accidental activity, which derives from its substance, but reaches out towards the other.

(2) The object of receptive knowledge must act upon and determine the subject. But we have seen that activity is something through which the agent posits in itself a new reality. Here, however, the objects puts this new reality not in itself, but in the subject. Yet in order to be a real activity, the reality posited by the agent must be its own. Thus in the present case we have an agent positing a reality of its own in the other,

realizing itself in the other. Spiritual activity, however, is self-realization in oneself. Hence in the present instance we have a case of non-spiritual activity, not of self-actuation in oneself but of self-actuation in the other.

It follows that, since as a being is so it acts, the objects which affect us in our everyday knowledge are non-spiritual or material objects.

(3) Moreover, the subject of such kind of knowledge must be material too. First, a being which receives an influence from without must have a capacity of reception, which allows the other to determine it. But the spirit determines itself. Thus beings endowed with outside receptivity must contain a non-spiritual principle through which the being is not self-present like a spirit, but outside of itself like a non-spiritual reality. This principle is materiality.

(4) Hence both the object and the subject of receptive knowledge are material. A finite spirit which knows the other as object through some influence deriving from the latter, must necessarily be a spirit in matter, a spirit endowed with the power of material receptivity, which we call *sensibility*. Thus we discover man's real essence. As a finite spirit he experiences not only the tension between virtual infinity and actual finiteness, but also the tension between (finite) spirit and matter. He is not endowed with sensibility because there is a world. Rather, there is a material world as man's world, because man is a finite spirit who knows receptively and because receptivity is possible only in materiality.

Materiality as a Principle

What we have said above allows us to determine more clearly the nature of materiality, which is called *prime matter* in the Aristotelian-Scholastic tradition.

(1) All material beings possess a principle of materiality. This principle itself is not material, it is not a being at all, but a principle of being, of material beings as such. Hence it cannot be known empirically, through scientific knowledge, but only metaphysically. In order to avoid all misconceptions, we shall, instead of using the term *prime matter,* which evokes too easily the idea of basic, raw materials, make use of the abstract term *materiality.*

Material beings stand in contrast with spiritual beings. The latter remain self-present in their activity, the former not. Thematically, we know material beings first, but only from without, through sense knowledge. That which is really known first, albeit unthematically, is spiritual being, which we experience directly as self-presence. It is only from this previous unthematic knowledge that the nature of material beings may be negatively explained as beings which are not spirit, which are not self-present. Hence materiality is the principle on account of which a being is non-spiritual, unable to be really self-present.

(2) It is not only on account of our manner of knowing, but also on account of the very nature of materiality, that we can interpret materiality only in a negative way. The nature of materiality is pure negativity. For spiritual self-presence in knowing and willing is the pure actuation of being as being, pure ontological perfection deriving from being as such. Hence when realized in its original purity, being is necessarily spirit. But if that which renders the spirit spirit is pure positivity of being as being, then that which makes the material being material must necessarily be pure negativity of non-being.

(3) Every negation is determined by that which it excludes. Essence excludes the presence of certain determinations or notes in a being. Materiality, on the other hand, excludes the perfection of spirituality. It is that determination in a finite being through which the latter is not spiritual, is unable to be self-

present. It is the principle on account of which a being is not self-present.

Being as being must be active, must actuate itself, by reaching out beyond itself towards the other. This other is not directly absolute being, it can only be another finite being. Hence the active being or agent is with the other through its activity. But a spiritual being is with the other while being with itself. On the other hand, a material being, when acting upon the other, does not return unto itself, it stays with the other, it loses itself in it. Materiality explains not only that a being is not self-present, but also that, in its activity, it is present with the other.

Not being self-present and being with the other go together. So we may call materiality that which causes a being to be outside of itself.

(4) It does not follow, however, that the spiritual being cannot be with the other when actuating itself consciously and freely in its other, for it is much more intensively with the other than material beings can be. The more it is present to itself, the more it has the power of being present with the other. We see this already in the vital processes of life, more so in the sense processes of the animal, but most clearly so in the intellectual activities of man, especially those by which he encounters other personal beings. Hence being present to oneself and being present to the other do not exclude each other. Yet this opposition rightly characterizes that which exists between spiritual and material beings. Even when present to the other the former is really self-present, while the latter is only present to the other and not with itself.

Matter and Form

(1) Materiality is that which causes a being to be outside of itself. A material being acts not in itself, but in the other. Hence its activity is in part determined by the other. But activity

derives from the being's essence. Hence the essence too of the material being is undetermined and needs further determination. This further determination must come from the other. Therefore, materiality is not only that which causes a being to be outside of itself, it is also and more originally the indetermination of the being's essence. But a finite essence, as we have explained, is the ontological possibility of a being. Hence materiality is the principle of the indetermination of a being's ontological possibility.

(2) Yet the finite being is not wholly undetermined, otherwise it could not exist. It possesses some determination. This possession supposes an element of determination in its essence, which combines with the element of indetermination. Insofar as, thus determined, it is posited in itself, we call it *substance*. A material being is one whose essence is composed of matter and form. Both together, as the undetermined determinable element, and as the determined determining element, constitute the essence. The being which has such an essence is a *material substance*.

(3) The doctrine of hylomorphism (from *hule* = matter and *morphè* = form) comes from Aristotle and was taken over from him by the Scholastics. Aristotle derived his idea of matter from natural philosophy and from logic. On the one hand, every formal, even a substantial change, presupposes a first undetermined element which remains throughout the change. On the other hand, in our daily speech, we always attribute predicates to a subject. If we take away all predicates from a subject, there must remain a first undetermined but determinable something, a substratum, which is prime matter.

The medieval Scholastics took over the ideas of form and prime matter, but not without modifications. While Thomas Aquinas held on to Aristotle's interpretation, Duns Scotus and Suarez, to mention only two names, considered prime matter as a first actuality, already determined, but in need of further determinations. The logical implication of this doctrine, fully worked out by Ockham, led that philosopher into nominalism.

The nature of prime matter can be grasped only if one understands it metaphysically, and not as one more object in nature. It is evident that that which makes the material being material, materiality as such, cannot be something positive. Should it be positive, it would be a perfection, it would be being. Being cannot limit itself. Hence materiality can only be negative, a mere potentiality. As such we must understand it metaphysically, not as some "raw material" or "stuff." That is why it might be better to speak of *materiality* rather than of *prime matter*. Materiality is a purely metaphysical element, a constitutive principle in the essence of the material being, not a first and underlying substratum.

Is there not a contradiction here? On the one hand, the material being is concretely determined by materiality. On the other hand, we call materiality the principle of indetermination within the being's essence. The apparent contradiction disappears when we recall that this indetermination determines the essence into not being spiritual. This is a negative determination, which derives from indetermination.

2. THE PERSONAL WORLD

I and the Other

Man is a finite spirit in materiality. He lives in a material world. In this world he meets not only material objects, but also and especially other persons. Man actuates himself not only in the things which he uses or makes, but also and mainly in the other spiritual beings, his fellow men, who communicate with him and appeal to his confidence and love.

Man can reach full self-development only in communion with other men. Others, especially the mother, have to help him reach self-awareness, especially through the medium of language. He succeeds in knowing himself as a person only by knowing other persons, who act somewhat like a mirror, in which, through "reflection," he discovers himself. Likewise, it is only by loving the others that he fulfills his own highest potentialities. Ancient and medieval philosophy have overlooked the primary importance of the person, because they were mainly interested in the universal and the general. Kant too paid scant attention to the person. Only recently, under the influence of such thinkers as Fichte, Scheler, Marcel, Buber, Brunner, and others, has the intersubjective dimension of man really come into its own in philosophy.

Freedom and Personal Behavior

The finite spirit actuates himself in the other through an identification of subject and object. If the identification takes place in the subject, we have knowledge. If it occurs in the object, we have an act of the will. It follows that the real nature of willing does not consist in grasping the values, but in responding to them, not in seizing the values *for me,* for my own enrichment and self-realization, but in welcoming them *in themselves,* for the sake of their own perfection. Relative values, which refer to a subject, may be grasped for the subject's sake. But absolute values, such as are not merely relative to the subject, but grounded in themselves, have to be welcomed in themselves and for their own sake. To will in this purest and fullest sense of the word is called *to love.*

Such absolute value is found in the spiritual-personal subject because he stands in the open horizon of being. It follows that the highest value-response, which consists in welcoming the value for its own sake, can take place only with respect to other spiritual-personal beings, in *personal love,* in the free Yes to the personal Thou, not for my own sake, but for his sake. The other person demands from me a total response which includes also his expression, what he communicates to me about himself. This expression too must be welcomed through faith and confidence in the other. Such is the condition of the possibility of *personal knowledge.* It allows the other to give me some access into his own personal life, as I stand open for his self-communication and thus manage to understand him.

On this highest level of knowledge, the knowledge of the other person, cognition and love, knowing and willing, influence each other. The more I know the other personally, the more I can love him. The more I love him, the better I understand him. This is so because of the ultimate unity of knowing and willing in the free self-actuation of the spirit.

The Necessity of Personal Involvement

(1) The ultimate sense of free donation in love follows from the metaphysical nature of man and from his metaphysical situation. Man has to realize himself through his free activity. As a finite being he stands in a basic relation to the absolute being of God. As a finite spirit he knows about this relation and he has to welcome it in knowledge and willing. The finite spirit, as actually finite and virtually infinite, is nothing but the possibility, freely to be realized, of the self-actuation of this relation to God. Only by transcending himself, by giving himself away to the other, can he fulfill his being. This self-transcending self-donation is possible for man only with respect to another being, who is himself fully personal and evokes man's personal love. Hence man's transcending dynamism towards God is the personal donation of one person to another person.

162

(2) Yet for man as a finite spirit in the world, the absolute being of God is not the immediate object of his self-actuation. Therefore, against the horizon of this ultimate goal, there arises another one which is limited and adapted to man: the material world as the first and immediate field of man's endeavor. Through the spiritual transcendence of his being, however, man always proceeds beyond his finite world horizon towards the infinite horizon of being. He does this especially by welcoming in love his fellow men, those other finite spirits which share materiality with him.

(3) Our attitudes towards other persons are ultimately attitudes with respect to an absolute value. Although really intending the other person, they aim, beyond him, at the absolute, insofar as they imply an absolute affirmation and self-donation which cannot go all the way in the finite person. Hence in their fullest extent they can be directed only towards God, and to the other person only insofar as we refer him to God. This does not mean that the other person is not worthy of our love in himself. His deepest self is precisely this relation to God, and we love him in his deepest self when our love refers him to God.

Morality

The personal free welcoming of other finite or infinite personal values constitutes the specific self-realization of man. We call such a personal self-realization, which occurs freely but in the line of human finality, a *moral* activity. This definition allows us to explain the nature of morality.

(1) Every finite being must operate in order to realize itself fully according to its nature. Operating is the self-actuation of a

being in reaching out to another. This other can enrich the agent because it is ontically good. Yet not every ontic good is equally valuable for all beings. The essence of the agent itself is the criterion which decides what beings constitute real values for it.

Man too must realize himself through his operation according to his nature. He must reach out towards another in his activity. His nature and his natural end decide what goods constitute real values for him. We call any value which refers not to a restricted range of human strivings, but to the whole of human self-development as human, a *moral* value. The ground and the norm of moral values, positive or negative, are to be found in man's essence itself, insofar as it is the principle of his self-realization. A free activity which grasps a moral value is thereby made into a *moral action*.

(2) Among all beings man is characterized by the fact that he possesses himself in knowledge and disposes of himself in freedom. His spiritual activities are essentially free. It is only when a moral value is freely welcomed and grasped that we have a moral action, through which man perfects himself in a spiritual and personal way. Hence a constitutive element of moral activity is *moral freedom*.

Yet man's freedom is not unrestricted. It is a conditioned freedom, made possible by previous conditions. Whenever a free action is performed, these conditions are necessarily, albeit un-thematically, co-willed. But the first and basic condition of freedom is *transcendence*. Because and insofar as man, as a finite spirit, acts in the unlimited horizon of being as such, hence in virtual dynamism towards the infinite, his activity passes beyond any determination by finite goods. He has freely to determine himself, and in every free determination he implicitly affirms his own transcendence. Man's most intimate willing aims at the absolute.

But God is not directly the object of a finite spirit's activity,

164

for then the finite spirit would have to be infinite. Hence man's basic volition must work itself out by striving towards objects in this world. A specific act of the will agrees or disagrees with the necessary basic volition. In the former case, it is to be performed, in the latter it is felt as forbidden. From the necessity of willing the absolute end in every volition, and from the freedom of willing or not willing specific objective goods, there derives, as a synthesis of this necessity and this freedom, the unconditioned obligation of the moral *ought*. We call the fact that human freedom is bound by the ought, *moral obligation*.

(3) The norm of morality lies in man's transcendent finality. It is not to be found in human essence considered as merely immanent, nor in man's ultimate end considered in isolation, but in man's concrete nature in its totality, that is, insofar as it is finalized towards the last and ultimate end, God himself.

Thus the basic moral activity consists in the freely consented self-donation to God, as mediated within this world through a similar donation to one's fellow man. For man, the highest value is the *personal* value, and all other values are values only insofar as they have some relation to the personal value.

Intersubjectivity

(1) The very nature of man's moral-personal self-realization entails a dialectical tension between his own and the other person's value as a person, between *Me* and *Thee*. On the one hand, moral self-realization consists essentially in the free acceptance of the other as a person. On the other hand, this acceptance is morally possible only if it does not involve a sacrifice of one's own personal value; otherwise, the acceptance and welcoming of the other would no longer be a means but an obstacle on the road towards the ultimate end of moral life.

165

Even the acceptance of another finite personal value must be subordinated to man's relation to the absolute.

(2) Hence there develops in intersubjective relations another tension, between *love* and *justice*. A moral action consists primarily in a personal acceptance of the other. But this must happen without giving up one's own personal value. It implies that he who acts morally possesses a realm of exclusive personal freedom, where he alone has to decide, which nobody else may take away from him or restrict, which he himself cannot give up. This exclusive realm of self-disposition is the realm of *personal rights*. Every person necessarily has a right to claim all that which is required by his final destination towards the absolute. It follows that man not only has the duty to safeguard the rights of others, but also to safeguard his own rights against the others, insofar as these rights are required as conditions of moral freedom.

(3) Thus man is caught in a multiplicity of intersubjective relationships. He is by nature made for togetherness [*Mitsein*] with others. It is only in this togetherness that he can fully develop as a person. Man is essentially a social being, destined to live in various groups. Groups in which love prevails over justice and right may be called *communities* [*Gemeinshaft*], whereas those where justice is the main connecting element are called *societies* [*Gesellschaft*].

(4) The personal and moral origin of human social relations allows us to determine the relation between the individual and the group. The ultimate purpose of the group is the personal realization of the individuals who comprise it. The individual can never be a mere means for the group; he is an end in himself, which even the group has to serve. On the other hand, the individual needs the group, since he can reach his full develop-

ment only by accepting and loving the others. He is what he has to be only when he proceeds beyond himself in will and deed, toward the higher totality of the group, endeavoring to bring about for the others too the best possible conditions for their personal development. In this respect, the group stands above the individual. Man's possibilities find in it a better field for their growth and unfolding. Hence between individual and society there is a reciprocal relation. The individual can be totally himself only when he is turned towards the group, and the group can be fully itself only when carried by free, responsible, and morally acting individuals, as it keeps aiming at the moral values and their realization by the individuals.

Historicity

The individual lives essentially in society and stands with it amidst the innerworldly, spatio-temporal, yet specifically human events which we call history. As much as he is a social being, man is a *historical* being. What is the nature of man's historicity?

(1) Man is a finite spirit in the material world. Through his body he takes part in the events of this world. Yet at the same time he transcends them through his spiritual nature, he is not wholly tied down to space and time, he can look back towards the past and forwards to the future. He reaches out to values which are unconditioned, standing above space and time. However, as spirit and body are not in man two distinct realms, as the body is the manifestation of the spirit and as the spirit must act in and through the body, there exists between *immanence* and *transcendence* an insuperable dialectical tension. In human activity the immanence is always already surpassed, and the transcendence is necessarily tied down to the immanent activity.

167

Only by operating within the world do we transcend the world.

(2) Within space and time the individual lives in a human society, he needs it for his own full development. But this society itself is a product of history, influenced both by the physical events in the cosmos and by the continual interaction of the individuals who are its members. The individual inserts himself in this personal and historically molded world, he adopts its manner of living and of thinking. Man possesses not only a *metaphysical a priori,* which is necessarily given with the nature of the spirit, but also an *empirical-historical a priori* which derives from the experience of the world, which is co-determined by historical events and which co-determines in its turn the concrete world-horizon of the indivdual. However, as the horizon of being exceeds the horizon of the world, as the metaphysical *a priori* encompasses and transcends the empirical-historical *a priori,* man can act in the historically developed world only by transcending it. Yet this transcending of the world is always rooted in an activity which occurs *in* it. Once more we meet the dialectic interaction of immanence and transcendence.

(3) It follows that history cannot be considered merely as the conditioning by time of the validity of all human judgments and evaluations. This view would not only overlook the transcendence of the human spirit; it would also fail to grasp the nature of history. History comprises two elements: immanence and transcendence, *historical necessity* and *personal freedom.* It is determined not only by the spatio-temporal changes in man's physical and social environment, but also and with equal necessity, by the transcendent dynamism of the spirit, which proceeds beyond all spatio-temporal conditions towards the unconditioned and absolute, whence it freely and creatively intervenes in the physical and social environment in which it is rooted.

It follows, moreover, that man's historicity does not take away his power of knowing the truth. It is true that, on account of the historically determined restriction of his world horizon, the individual can never grasp the whole truth, but only partial aspects of it. However, as human thinking occurs always and necessarily in the horizon of being, every act of it co-contains unthematically, as a condition of its possibility, the basic knowledge about being and about the principles and structures of being. However, their explicitation supposes empirical mediation, which is once more conditioned by time and history. Man's world is always *transcendent and transparent for being.* Every historical period is transcendent and transparent for suprahistorical, unconditionally valid truth. That is why metaphysics is possible at all times; but at all times it has to be reconstructed from out of its then historical context. This is possible only if man freely opens up for the truth. Because the spirit's freedom breaks out of the confines of world, time, and history, it is only by a free commitment that man may reach suprahistorical truth.

VII.

BEING IN THE PRIMORDIAL ACT

THROUGHOUT our study of metaphysics we have met references to absolute Being. A metaphysical investigation of being, which studies beings in their being, according to the laws of being, can reach its goal only if it advances all the way to absolute "being itself." It is time, therefore, to put together in a definite order the insights which have hitherto referred us from multiplicity to unity, from the conditioned to the unconditioned, from finite beings to the infinite being.[1] They constitute the metaphysical foundation of a philosophical theology which will not, in this book, be fully worked out but whose main lines will be laid down. The doctrine of being has its peak in the doctrine of God, as the latter finds its foundation in the doctrine of being. Metaphysics as the science of beings as beings finds its fulfillment only when it turns into a science of the divine Being. And metaphysics as the science of the divine Being is possible only when it derives from the science of beings as such. Both aspects are complementary, they possess—as Aristotle has said—their unity in metaphysics. Their final conclusion, which is also the highest achievement of human knowledge, is the metaphysical knowledge of being in the divine primordial Act.

[1] Hence we cannot help repeating many things which have already been mentioned previously.

1. THE EXISTENCE OF GOD

The Necessity of Being

(1) Insofar as it is, a being is necessarily itself; insofar as it is, it cannot not be, or be something else. This necessity is co-known and co-affirmed by us in all of our questions about beings, in all of our knowledge of them, as a condition of the possibility of such questions and of such knowledge. Further, this necessity constitutes the ontic principle of identity, or, in its negative formulation, the ontic principle of contradiction. Previous to it, however, and implied by it as its very ground and foundation, is the ontological principle of identity, or, negatively formulated, the ontological principle of contradiction. Being is necessarily being; being cannot not be, it necessarily excludes non-being.

It follows at once that in our every act of thinking there is co-posited and presupposed the primordial realization of the necessity of absolute being. This is not yet thematically a knowledge of the absolute being of God, since the absolute and necessary character of being is not yet contrasted with the finite and conditioned beings. At first we have only a general and undetermined knowledge, a basic unavoidable assertion: being as such cannot not be, being as such is absolute. Within this assertion the knowledge about the absolute being of God is already co-posited, but it becomes thematic only when we have shown that no finite being is being itself, that every finite being is distinct from absolute being, since it possesses being only in a conditioned and restricted manner. However, since, insofar as it is, the finite being necessarily is, it presupposes, beyond itself, the absolutely necessary being, being itself.

It might be objected that the necessity of being expressed in the principle of identity is only a hypothetical necessity. "If"

171

something is, it necessarily is. From this principle we may not yet deduce the necessary reality of absolute being. To this argument we reply that hypothetical necessity necessarily presupposes and includes apodictical necessity. For the connection expressed in this hypothetical principle is no longer hypothetical, but apodictically necessary. If something is, it necessarily is. The connection between the antecedent and the consequent is no longer conditional, but absolute. It is true that this connection is only a logical one, a connection between essences. From it we are not allowed to deduce the necessity of real being. But this logical or essential connection presupposes the necessity of real being, in which the logical connection is rooted. Should being not first be real, there would be no essences and no logical connections between them. Every essential or logical connection presupposes the apodictical necessity of being.

(2) Yet this certitude does not yet give us explicitly any knowledge about the absolute being of God. We must rather show that the finite existent is not the necessary and necessarily affirmed being itself, that it is distinct from the latter, because it presupposes being itself as its unconditioned condition, as the condition of its own hypothetical necessity. For the world of our experience is filled with many beings which are conditioned and finite, thus presupposing the unity, necessity, and infinity of being itself.

(a) The dynamism of our intellect meets many realities as beings. One is not the other, each differs from the others, although the others too *are*. Beings show multiplicity and diversity. But multiplicity presupposes unity, diversity presupposes community. It is only on the basis of previous unity that the many can be grasped as a multiplicity. Likewise, diversity presupposes the unity of some community in diversity. It is only on account of a community, previous to the diversity, that the single elements can set themselves up and differentiate themselves in their multiplicity. Otherwise, they would fall apart in wholly unconnected alterity, they would no longer stand in the relation of diversity. Hence when we know of things as many and diverse, we can do so only if we know of their previous unity and community.

(b) When something is posited among many other things, we discover further that it is *conditioned*. We know, of course, that, insofar as it is, every being is unconditionally; when we state that "this is so," we posit the state of affairs unconditionally, not merely as valid for us, or for a restricted circle of beings, but universally for the unlimited totality of being. Yet we know that a being *is* unconditionally only *if* posited in being. Hence it is conditionally unconditioned, not necessarily necessary. That is: once it is posited it refers not only to a (not necessary) condition, which is in its turn conditioned, but also to an unconditioned (simply necessary) condition. It follows that the conditionally unconditioned is possible only under an unconditional condition. The unconditional affirmation of a conditioned reality is possible only under condition of a simply unconditioned presupposition. Thus the conditionally unconditioned presupposes—if we may say so—something which is unconditionally unconditioned. That which is relatively necessary presupposes something which is absolutely necessary. When we know about a being that *is*, we know that it is unconditionally, although we are aware that it is conditioned. But we can know that the conditioned exists unconditionally only through some anticipating knowledge of the unconditioned condition under which it is posited and by which it is made into something conditionally unconditioned. Therefore, the mind's dynamism can reach the existent in its unconditioned validity only if it always anticipates the simply unconditioned; the intellectual dynamism, through which we grasp being in its unconditional validity, is possible only on the basis of the intellectual anticipation of the simply unconditioned within whose horizon we are able to know beings in their conditioned unconditionality.

(c) But the horizon of unconditioned validity is necessarily the unlimited horizon of being as such. Only an unlimited horizon can give rise to absolute validity. But the beings which we reach in knowledge and inquiry within this horizon are *finite.* As such, they can never exhaust the infinity of the horizon of being. The dynamism of our mind proceeds necessarily beyond every finite object, beyond the sum of all possible finite objects, towards the infinite itself. It can reach its fulfillment only in the unlimited. But the unlimited towards which our dynamism keeps striving—in knowledge and inquiry—is not an infinity within finiteness; for such an infinite would still be potential infinity within actual finiteness. It is an infinity *before* or *above* all the finite; for only in this way can it exist as actual infinity, that is, as the real fullness of all the infinite possibilities of being.

Hence all our knowing and inquiring presupposes, as the condition of its possibility, the basic knowledge and affirmation of being in its unconditioned necessity. But the beings of our experience are not necessary, they are distinct from necessary being and presuppose it. Hence our knowledge of being, which constitutes the condition of all our knowledge about beings, proceeds beyond all finite beings towards the absolute and infinite being.

(3) We start our examination of the proofs for the existence of God with this consideration of our basic knowledge of the necessity of being, because this unthematic knowledge and affirmation of being underlies all other demonstrations of God and is made explicit in them. It is clear in what sense we admit an *immediate knowledge of God.* It is not in the sense of a thematic explicit knowledge, nor in the sense of an immediate intuition of God. Our explicit knowledge of God needs the mediation of the world, which we know and which we transcend in our knowledge. This knowing and transcending is possible only on account of an unthematic anticipation, through which we unconsciously reach out towards the Absolute. All of our knowledge contains an original immediate knowledge of the necessary and absolute character of being. But this character is already

implicitly the necessity of absolute Being itself. The latter is known explicitly when it has been distinguished from the finite beings, when we have discovered that the beings, in their multiplicity, relativity, and finiteness, are not themselves the being which is necessary and necessarily always already affirmed but presuppose this being beyond themselves. Thus it is only through the mediation of the finite beings of experience that we discover that the necessity of being is distinct from them as the absolutely other, as absolute Being. Nevertheless, it follows from all of this that the knowledge of God does not really represent a passage of our mind to something hitherto wholly unknown, but only an explicitation and development of our knowledge of the necessity of being. Thus it seems to be more correct not to speak of an immediate knowledge of God but only of an immediate knowledge of the necessary and absolute nature of being. To show that this necessary being is not the finite world of our experience, but only God, who infinitely surpasses this world, requires further steps in our argumentation.

(4) Thus we get a first idea of the further proofs of God. The necessary being is distinguished from the finite beings because the latter are many, conditioned, and finite, thus presupposing being itself as one, unconditioned, and infinite. In the following proofs we further explain the relation between the many and the one, the conditioned and the unconditioned, the finite and the infinite. The finite being of our experience is contingent, hence it demands the Absolute Being as its first cause, that is, it stands with respect to the Absolute Being in a relation of causal dependence. This relation was already implied in our previous considerations; it will be made explicit in the *argument from causality*. The human mind, which in all its inquiring and knowing about beings affirms the necessity of Being itself, manifests in this way a dynamism which strives beyond the finite and whose ultimate goal is the absolute and infinite Being. In other words, whenever it knows a finite being it stands with

respect to the Absolute Being in a relation of finality, which will be made explicit in the *proof from finality*.

Thus we have basically—although not exclusively—three demonstrations of God, corresponding to the three ontological principles of identity, causality, and finality. In the first proof we have shown that the principle of identity, which underlies our every act of thinking as a condition of its possibility, presupposes the primordial affirmation of the necessity of being. The second proof shows that, according to the principle of causality, every finite and contingent being demands the Absolute Being as its first cause. The third proof will show how, according to the principle of finality, each finite being is referred to the Absolute Being as to its ultimate goal.

The Cause of the World

(1) The beings have shown through their multiplicity, relativity, and finiteness that they do not constitute the absolutely necessary being itself. They are contingent, by themselves they may be or not be. We shall briefly examine a few criteria of this contingency.

(a) A being is contingent whenever it stands *in the flux of becoming,* when it begins and ceases to exist, thus showing that it is not necessary. However, the number of beings which we can thus see ceasing or starting to exist is quite limited. As a rule, we notice only changes in the things, not a real new becoming or a total disappearing. Yet, this criterion may be used, especially within the domain of living beings, where reproduction brings forth new organisms, which eventually stop existing, thus clearly manifesting their contingency.

But we experience in the most direct manner the contingency of our own Ego. We ourself have not always existed. We have emerged from non-being, we have been thrown into existence, we know that we were not, that we are not necessarily in existence, that we have not entered into existence by ourself. We know about the contingency of our own existence.

(b) The domain of contingency widens when we add a second criterium, that of *temporality*. Whatever exists in this world stands in time, in the steady flow of succession, proceeding from the past over the present towards the future. It possesses its existence not all at once in a permanent now, but in a steady change and succession of moments relaying each other in time. Each one of these moments comes and goes, it is contingent. But if a being's existence consists of the succession of such moments of time, the existence of that being itself is contingent.

(c) The domain of contingency extends further when we consider its metaphysically ultimate criterium: *finiteness*. All beings of our experience are finite, they are, but they are not being itself and as a whole. They might be better, more valuable, more perfect. They are limited by other beings. They are composed of being and essence, and the union of these two is contingent.

(2) But if a contingent being exists, it demands a *cause*. This follows from the principle of causality, which we have established above. This cause might itself be a finite, contingent cause, which would in its turn require another cause. Should the latter too be contingent, we must go on to a further cause. But a series of contingent causes, even if we suppose that it goes on indefinitely, remains contingent and explains neither itself nor the beings which constitute it.

Moreover, we suppose here that a finite and contingent cause is capable of producing beings as beings. But that is impossible. To produce beings as beings supposes a cause whose formal object is being as being, which is therefore capable of producing absolutely all beings, of realizing all the possibilities of being. No finite cause is capable of this realization; only the infinite first cause possesses this power, this omnipotence.

177

Hence finite beings suppose a first cause, which can be none other than Absolute and Infinite Being itself.

The Final End of the Spirit

(1) We can know and inquire about God only because our intellect, although immersed in the world of experience, transcends this world towards the absolute and infinite being. As we have mentioned above, we grasp beings in their multiplicity, which supposes some previous knowledge of their unity. We grasp them as conditioned, which presupposes some knowledge of the Unconditioned. We grasp them as finite which would be impossible without some pre-knowledge of infinite being. Hence if we know beings as beings, this supposes that we know them in the unlimited horizon of being, it supposes the virtual infinity of our spirit, which, beyond every finite existent, reaches out towards being as a whole, and whose capacity can be filled only through the actual infinity of absolute being. We experience the dynamism of our intellect towards unity beyond all multiplicity, towards the unconditioned beyond everything conditioned, towards the infinite past all finiteness. This dynamism reveals to us as the final end or goal of the finite spirit the one, unconditioned, and infinite being. This dynamism makes sense only if it is directed towards such a goal. This goal is an *a priori* condition of the possibility of the undeniable striving of the human spirit.

(2) But such a striving, which constitutes the very essence of our mind, cannot head towards nothingness. Its end must at least be possible. We are endowed with the spiritual power of knowing. Hence spiritual knowledge is possible, for the power of knowing implies its possibility. But this power has been shown to have a constitutive finality towards the absolute and infinite being. Thus the act must be possible by which the spirit

reaches absolute and infinite being, and the act is possible only if its content, *in casu,* absolute being itself, is possible; otherwise, the striving of the spirit, as it really is, would be contradictory.

(3) But if the absolute being is possible, it is also necessarily real. In the present case, and only in it, may we conclude from the possibility to the reality, provided only that the possibility in question is not a mere logical possibility, but the real possibility of being. Hence we do not conclude from a conceivable, non-contradictory *concept* of God to his reality. This would be an invalid conclusion. But we start from the real activity of the spirit, which is possible only if it aims at a really possible end, the absolute being. And the latter is possible only as *being itself,* which subsists no longer in the duality of being and essence, but whose essence it is to be, whose being is its essence. Being itself is its essence; therefore, it is the absolutely necessary being, which by its very essence cannot not be; it is the infinite fullness of being, in which all the possibilities of being are necessarily realized. Since its essence is to be, it would no longer be possible if it were merely possible and not real. In that case, its very essence would be suppressed. Hence if the absolute being is possible, it is also real. But we have shown that the possibility of the absolute being is a condition of the possibility of the activity of the spirit, as it strives towards the absolute. Hence the Absolute Being really exists.

(4) In the line of our approach, the above proof might be formulated in a simple and briefer way as follows: The question presupposes the possibility of an answer. But our question is an unlimited one, since we may inquire about everything and continue to inquire beyond any possible limits. By its very nature, the question aims at the infinity of all that which is knowable. Therefore, the act of inquiring presupposes the possibility of an infinite answer, which puts an end to all questions. But neither a finite being nor the totality of all finite beings can

supply an infinite answer and put an end to an unlimited inquiry. Therefore, the question presupposes something infinite, which, insofar as it is knowable, may supply an infinite answer. But, as we have shown, the possibility of the infinite necessarily implies its reality. Hence the act of inquiring presupposes the reality of the absolute, infinite being.

(5) Other proofs of God may be devised. Every finite being stands in a fundamental relation to the absolute being of God. When we render this relation explicit, we may derive from it a proof of God's existence. Thus demonstrations of God are possible from the finalistic order and harmony of the world, from the finite subject-object relation, hence also from the ontic truth and goodness of beings, further from the absolute nature of moral obligation, from the transcendence of human society and history, from the religious experience both of the individual and of humanity as a whole, and so on.

In all of these proofs we start from something which is really given in experience, never from a pure concept. We show then that the finite existent, as given to us in experience, presupposes, as a condition of its possibility, the absolute being of God, that it can be understood only under this condition. The proof may use not only the principle of causality, but also the principle of finality, as we have done above. It may even proceed in a simpler way, and arrive at God from the relation of that which is conditioned to its condition, without having to show that such a condition has to be an efficient cause.

All demonstrations of God's existence are ultimately based upon the *transcendence of the spirit*. It is only because and insofar as the finite spirit operates in the horizon of being as such, because it possesses an essential relation to the absolute and infinite being, that in every one of its spiritual activities it always already transcends the conditioned towards the unconditioned, the finite towards the infinite. Thus whenever we wish critically to reduce a proof of God's existence to the ultimate conditions of its possibility, we must, by means of transcendental reflection, render thematic the essential transcendence of the human spirit. Or the other way around: Whenever through reflection we make explicit the metaphysically transcendent nature of the human spirit, we have a proof of God's existence—or rather we have *the* proof of God's existence, which is the ground and foundation of all the other demonstrations.

2. GOD'S ESSENCE

Analogical Knowledge of God

(1) Finite and contingent beings presuppose the absolute and infinite being. The question arises, however, whether we can reach a positive conceptual knowledge of the absolute. The answer can only come from a consideration of the principle of analogy.

The question about being proceeds beyond any single and finite being, it is never put to rest as long as it discovers only finite beings. This quest gives rise to the dynamism and the dialectics of analogy, as a movement of the spirit which transcends every limited and conceptual knowledge of being not by denying it, but by passing beyond it, by refusing to accept it as the final answer. Since the horizon of being is unlimited, this movement heads for the infinite. In this movement every new object is being, not something which accrues to being from without, but something through which being further unfolds itself from within. Whatever *is* shares being, not in a univocal, but in an analogous way. Whatever is refers beyond itself to the pure fullness of being itself.

(2) If finite being itself is not univocal but analogous, *a fortiori* it stands in a *relation of analogy with respect to the absolute being*. Absolute being is not a being among beings. It

is the ground and foundation of all beings and it does not subsist on the same level with them. Yet it is not altogether unlike these beings, the term *being* is not equivocally applied to it, as to something utterly different. Otherwise, it could not be the ground and foundation of all beings. As ground and foundation it has an analogous relation of similarity and otherness, of sameness and difference, with respect to the finite beings. The absolute *is*, but in a manner which infinitely surpasses the manner of being of all finite existents.

The absolute is not only the ground and foundation of all beings; it is also the first, unconditioned condition of the horizon of being, within which the spirit, in knowledge and volition, actuates itself as it reaches out for being. It is the unconditioned *whereunto* of the movement of the finite spirit. It follows once more that it cannot be an object within the horizon of possible objects, it does not stand in a relation of univocity with the finite beings. Neither can it be totally different from beings, and only equivocally called being. As the unconditioned condition of all inquiring about being, it can stand only in a relation of analogy with respect to finite beings, having something in common with them, yet essentially different from them.

Since it is not a being among beings, not an object within the horizon of possible objects, it can never directly in itself become an object of knowledge, the absolute cannot be represented or conceived in the way of a being. But since, as the constitutive element of the horizon of being, it is that whereunto the whole dynamism of the finite spirit always and necessarily keeps heading, every act of knowing and of willing ultimately aims at it.

(3) Every finite being *is*, but it is within certain limits. The absolute, on the other hand, is *being itself*, the infinite fullness of all the possibilities of being. We grasp all beings in their limited being. But when the transcendent movement of our spirit heads for the Absolute, we may drop and transcend the

limitations, through a *negation of the negation,* thus intending the pure positivity of an unlimited perfection. Each such un-limited perfection is realized in the absolute being of God, they are all infinitely unified in him. Hence we must attribute to God all pure perfections of being. We reach him in the pure positivity of his being, but never as pure positivity, but only through the medium of a *negation of the negation.* It follows again that we possess of God no direct and adequate concept, but only an analogous and inadequate one.

(4) The problem remains, however, how a pure perfection of being may be known as such, whether and how it is possible to distinguish that which is posited through the pure perfection as such and that which derives from the finite limitation. Should this distinction be impossible to make, we would be unable to make assertions about God having a positive even though only analogous content.

But it is a fact that in all our inquiring and knowing we are in touch with the pure positivity of being. Being belongs to all that about which we inquire and know; being as being knows of no limits, it is the principle of pure positivity. But an activity which reaches being as being is possible only because, of itself, it has an unlimited range. A spirit which strives towards being as being has an infinite capacity. While remaining, in itself, a finite spirit, it possesses an infinite capacity, dynamism, and range. That is why man has some inkling of what pure perfec-tions are in themselves, although he may never grasp them con-ceptually as pure perfections. That is why he really knows God, although he can never enclose him in a concept or a definition. Whatever he *conceives* about God is hopelessly inadequate, yet what he basically *means* or *intends* through his concepts comes up to some extent, dynamically not statically, to what the Absolute really **is.**

183

Absolute Being

(1) God is being itself. In him, being is no longer assumed and limited by an essence distinct from it, it exists in fullness in itself. Being itself is absolutely necessary, it cannot not be, its essence is to be, it excludes the possibility of not being.

Being as being is *infinite,* all perfections of being are fully realized in it. Being as being includes no limits, it is a principle of mere positivity and actuality; it contains no limiting essence, hence it is the infinite fullness of all the infinite possibilities of being.

(2) It follows, moreover, that absolute being is necessarily absolutely *simple.* A being is simple when it contains no parts, when it cannot be divided. But absolute being is essentially the fullness of being and of all perfections of being. Thus in absolute being, being and essence and all perfections of being are absolutely identical. Absolute being contains no parts, it is indivisible. Should there be parts in it, one of them would not be another. There would be a metaphysical possibility of division. The absolute would be contingent. The parts would limit each other, hence be limited, finite. But a being composed of finite parts is essentially finite. Therefore, the absolute being is the infinite fullness of being in absolutely simple unity.

As absolutely simple, the absolute is also *immutable.* For every change supposes a real difference between a steady, unchanging element and one which is added or subtracted. Such a difference cannot exist in the absolutely simple being. Furthermore, change cannot go together with infinity, for it means either an increase or a decrease in being or perfection. It supposes that the changing subject does not possess all perfection, that it is limited in perfection. Therefore, the infinite being is immutable.

If the absolute is immutable, it is also *supratemporal.* It does not exist in the flux and succession of time, but as an everlasting now. Whatever exists in time is contingent. That which was, no longer is. That which will be, is not yet. That which is, was not previously and will no longer be afterwards. Every moment of such a being's existence becomes and ceases to exist. Its whole being is becoming and vanishing. It is not necessary, but contingent. Hence the absolutely necessary being is not in time, it is supratemporal, it possesses its whole being as an immutable, everlasting now. Absolute being is also *supraspatial*, for, if it existed in space, it would be extended, composed of parts, and no longer absolutely simple.

(3) From all of this it follows that the primordial being is absolutely *transcendent* with respect to the material, spatio-temporal world and with respect to all finite beings. Contradictory attributes of which one is the negation of another, cannot really be identical. But between finite being and the absolute being there exist contradictory attributes: contingence and necessity, finiteness and infinity, simplicity and composition, mutability and immutability, existence in time and not in time, in space and not in space. Hence finite being is not identical with infinite being. Nor can it—either as its mode (Spinoza) or as its moment (Hegel)—be partially identical with infinite being as a finite way of self-development or self-realization of the absolute. This would render the absolute finite, even though potentially infinite; it would do away with the infinity of the absolute. This would introduce into the absolute partial aspects in which it would actuate itself, and this would do away with the simplicity and the infinity of the absolute. Therefore, the absolute is not identical with, but different from and transcendent with respect to all infinite beings. It is the infinitely other, infinitely exceeding all finite beings, never entering immanently into them, but forever remaining transcendent as the pure actuality of being.

Absolute Spirit

(1) The absolute being is the infinite fullness of being, the primordial identity of being with itself. Finite beings are not self-identical, but self-identifying. In their activity they strive towards self-identity. The absolute being is fully self-identical, self-identified, self-identity, and this active self-identity is the supremely pure form of *activity*. It is an activity which implies no change, no passage from one state to another. It is activity that is identical with absolute being, it is infinitely perfect self-subsistent activity.

(2) It is an activity which does not reach out to another being, since the infinite being cannot actuate itself in another, in a finite being. It is rather an identity which we have to conceive as returning unto the acting subject itself, actuating it in perfect self-identity. It is not a transient or transitive activity, which posits an object distinct from the subject, but an immanent activity, which actuates the acting subject itself as the object of the activity. Such inner activity is called *life*. Hence the absolute being is not only infinite activity but also *infinite life*. It is a life that infinitely surpasses all finite life and realizes to the fullest extent all the possibilities of life.

(3) Living activity which is not bound to a conditioned and limited horizon, which occurs in the unconditioned and illimited horizon of being, is spiritual activity, and manifests the duality of knowing and willing. Therefore, as infinite life the absolute is infinite spiritual activity and, as such, *infinite knowledge*. It is a knowledge which is not distinct from absolute being, but which is simply identical with it. The absolute is therefore the self-subsistent infinite fullness of knowing, which exhausts all the possibilities of knowing and actually knows all the knowable. An infinite activity of knowing can have as its object only the

infinite being itself. Hence infinite knowledge is the infinitely perfect and exhaustive self-knowing of the absolute spirit who, in the identity of subject and object, luminously comprehends its own infinite truth in infinite knowledge. Since every finite being has the ground of its possibility in the absolute, it is always already known in God's infinite knowledge.

(4) Spiritual activity is both knowing and willing. Since the absolute, as absolute spirit, is the pure primordial spiritual activity, it is not only subsistent infinite knowing, but also subsistent *infinite willing*. Infinite willing, too, is not distinct from and added to infinite being, but coincides fully with it. The absolute is therefore the perfect identity of being, knowing, and willing. It is subsistent volition, which exhaust all possibilities of willing, which embraces all goodness, all that which may be willed. The object of absolute willing can only be absolute being. Therefore, absolute willing is the self-willing and self-loving of God who, in full identity of subject and object, welcomes his own infinite goodness in infinite willing and love. Since each finite being holds its foundation in God, every one of them is posited in its goodness by the infinite will.

(5) It does not follow, however, that the finite beings are *necessarily* posited in being by the infinite will. God loves necessarily only his own infinite goodness; he loves the being of finite existents *freely*. Since this being is finite and contingent, it cannot force the infinite will to realize it. Moreover, although every finite being is possible, all of them together are not co-possible, they are not possible together. The realization of one may exclude that of another. Therefore, the positing by God of the finite beings is an act of *infinite freedom*.

When finite beings exist, they have simply been transferred from non-being into being, they have been *created*. Such an activity is the exclusive prerogative of God. For it implies the positing of being as being, its formal object is being, it extends to all possible reality, its material object is all possible beings. Such an activity supposes omnipotence and infinity.

Even after finite beings have been created by God's free activity, they remain essentially contingent. Even while they *are,* they might also not have been. Hence they must be maintained in being by God. This activity is traditionally known as *conservation,* which is nothing but continued creation, by which the absolute being keeps the finite beings in being.

(6) Absolute being is absolute spirit, hence also *absolute person.* For a person, who may be defined as a spiritual subject (*suppositum*), must possess the ontological perfections of the spirit and must be fully autonomous like a single complete substance. But the absolute being is absolute spirit and exists fully, autonomously in itself, as a substance. It does so, however, not as a categorial substance, as we meet that substance in our experience, but as a supracategorial one, in a sense which is analogous with respect to finite substances. Absolute being possesses unity and simplicity, hence it is an individual substance. But it is not an individual substance among many others. It exists previous to and as the foundation of all multiplicity. It is individual only in an analogous sense. Absolute being is substance in the fullest sense of the word, and, as fullness of being, it cannot be assumed or taken over by some other, by some finite being. Thus it possesses the full autonomy and independence which is required by a *subject* or *suppositum.*

Therefore, we must say of God that he is a person, albeit in an analogous sense. He transcends infinitely all the depth and richness of human personality, not by suppressing them, but by "sublating" or sublimating them in his own divine personality.

(7) Hence philosophy can really reach a *personal God.* Too often the objection is heard that philosophy arrives only at a lifeless *ens a se,* at some impersonal absolute, at a faceless first cause. This is not quite true. When we reach God, philosophi-

cally, we reach him necessarily as the absolute being, that is, as the absolute and infinite fullness of being and of all the perfections of being. These include life, spiritual and personal life, knowledge and will, love and freedom. Since all of these perfections are pure perfections, they are not suppressed by being, but realized to an infinite extent, they are sublated to sublime proportions. They must be predicated of God in a positive, albeit analogical sense. God is the infinitely living and personal God.

It is true, however, that philosophy alone does not put us in personal contact with this living and personal God. This God freely comes out to meet us, reveals himself to us, and makes us capable of bridging the infinite distance which separates us from him.

3. MAN AND GOD

The Essential Relation to God

Every finite being stands in an essential relationship to the being of God. We may distinguish three aspects in it.

(1) The first aspect is that of exemplary causality. God is the *primordial model* of every finite being. The absolute being is the infinite fullness of being in whom all perfections of being exist in perfect purity. The finite being is posited as a possible because its pure perfections pre-exist eminently in God, its limiting essence is formally projected in divine knowledge. It is therefore a finite copy of the infinite divine model.

(2) When, however, a being exists in reality, it stands in a relation of efficient causality with respect to God. God is the *first cause* of all finite beings. All contingent beings are brought about by God's free volition, they are transferred from non-existence to existence, they are created by God.

(3) This contingency entails a relation of finality between the finite being and God. God is the *last end* of all finite beings. A spiritual being can act freely and consciously only for an end. The same is true also of God. But God cannot operate for a finite end; this would make him dependent on a finite reality. His end must be infinite and it can only be God's infinite being itself. Therefore, God can will finite beings only for his own sake. His end is not something which he has to reach, it can only be something which he wishes to communicate, to share with others. Thus the finite being exists in order to reproduce and to express as perfectly as possible, although always in a finite and deficient way, the infinite perfection of God. Hence the ultimate end of all finite beings is God himself, even though, as we shall show presently, this end can be reached only in or through the finite spirit.

The Spirit's Relation to God

Every finite being stands in an essential relation to God. But not all finite beings can consciously realize and actuate this relation. Within this world only man is capable of doing so. When he is self-aware and when he freely disposes of himself, he fulfills himself knowingly and freely in the horizon of being as such, towards the absolute being of God.

(1) This ability to fulfill itself presupposes that the finite spirit is essentially *transcendent*. We have sufficiently established this transcendence in the previous chapters. It supposes, moreover, that the finite spirit is *free*. He has freely to accept and to fulfill what he is already by his very nature, a being open to infinity, transcending all of the finite realities towards God. The more man gets out of himself, transcends himself towards the infinite, the more he fulfills his own nature and becomes what he really is and has to be.

190

(2) The first step in this direction consists in *knowledge* of God. Man should freely yield to the dynamism of his own mind which leads him beyond all finite realities to the infinite being of God. But knowledge is only the first step. Through it the subject draws the object within itself, gets in touch with the object as it is in him, not as it is in itself. In order to reach the object as it is in itself, willing or volition is required, which makes the subject yield to the object and find himself again in the object as the latter is in itself. That is why knowledge alone does not grasp values, it not yet a value-response. Man's real contact with God occurs through *willing and volition,* through *love.*

(3) Free volition through which man realizes and actuates himself according to his nature is called *moral activity.* Man is capable of it only because he transcends every finite being in the direction of God. It is this transcendence which allows man to will or not to will the finite objects, which makes him free. It is this transcendence which renders some finite tasks obligatory insofar as they are necessary means for man to reach his transcending end. In all of his moral activities man is unthematically aware of this transcendence.

(4) More than through knowledge and through moral activity, transcendence is freely and personally acknowledged in man's *religious attitude.* This attitude consists in man's freely and explicitly turning towards God. It supposes that man acknowledges God. Acknowledging is more than mere knowledge, it implies an act of free welcoming and admitting of the reality of God, some kind of self-donation of man to God, therefore some activity of the will.

But it is an act of the will through which man does not try to grasp something for himself, but one through which he welcomes and admits the highest, unconditioned, infinite value for its own sake. It is an act of willing as applied to a personal value, *in casu* to the absolute, infinite personal value of God. This is the loftiest possible reaction of the will, so that it often produces repercussions in man's feelings, thus permeating his entire psycho-physical personality. However, this total reaction is not essential, but only man's conscious and free yielding to the appeal of the Infinite.

The religious attitude is therefore the highest and most fully human attitude of man. It is not a purely rational or intellectualistic reaction, as Spinoza would have it. Nor is it merely a concern of the will, as Kant said. Both knowledge and will are involved in it, it does not originate below or above them in some *irrational* domain of man, in the realm of mere feeling or sentiment, as Friedrich Schleiermacher, William James, and some modernists suggested. It includes both knowledge and will and it often is suffused by intensely human feeling. The knowledge is not purely cerebral but in intimate contact with the will and with love; the willing is not a blind imperative, but guided by some kind of more or less explicit or thematic knowledge. Feeling is not essential, although, whenever it is present, it makes of the religious attitude the most complete of man's attitudes.

Philosophy and Religion

From the nature of philosophy we may find out its relation to religion. Religion is more comprehensive and original than philosophy. The latter is born from religion, it is ordained towards religion in which it finds its fulfillment. Religion is the "immediacy" of an integral personal attitude towards God. When we rationalize it through reflection, philosophy turns into a "mediation" of religion. Its nature and meaning is not to do away with religion, but to transform it into a "mediated immediacy," so that the religious attitude, after having been deepened and enriched by rational reflection, becomes once more direct and immediate.

(1) Religion is more comprehensive than philosophy. The latter remains essentially restricted to theoretical knowledge, even though this knowledge may refer to the unlimited totality of being. It is not restricted in its range of objects, but it is incomplete in its manner of grasping these objects. In this sense, willing and acting reach farther than knowing. So does religion, which, conditioned by knowledge, molds and encompasses the practical volitions, the moral activity, and the external life of man.

It is true that every religion, be it ever so primitive, contains a theoretical element. Religious attitudes and activity suppose some kind of awareness of the world's dependence on God. But this awareness does not have to be reflectively rational. As a rule, the psychological and historical origin of religions is to be found more frequently in myths than in reasoning, in images than in concepts. Yet even these myths and these images vaguely hint at an explanation of reality through its relation to God.

(2) But man's spontaneous religious attitude quite naturally gropes for some philosophical reflection. Man wishes to be reflexively sure of his position in the universe and with respect to the Absolute. He begins to examine the theoretical foundations of religion. This investigation may lead to a conflict between philosophy and religion. On the one hand, philosophical thought is tempted to consider itself as absolute and to take over the whole of life. Since this does not succeed, since there is more to life than rational certitude, life evades the grasp of philosophy and the latter turns to problems which are alien to life. On the other hand, concrete life and religion shun such an esoteric philosophy and give up the attempt to discover a solid

193

theoretical basis and justification. Thus philosophy and religion grow apart not on account of anything in their own nature, but as a result of extreme positions assumed by both of them: extreme rationalism of philosophy and extreme irrationalism of religion.

(3) However, when philosophy and religion are understood according to their real nature, they can and should agree. On the one hand, philosophy reaches its scope only when it can answer the questions which concern man as a whole and in the innermost core of his being. It is able to do this only when it reaches out towards the fullness of being and its ultimate foundation, that is, towards God, in whom alone man's metaphysical restlessness may find peace. Hence philosophy reaches its full sense only as metaphysics and as philosophy of religion.

On the other hand, religion should receive from philosophy assurance, depth, and enrichment. It is true that religion is more than philosophy, that life implies more than thinking or knowing. But in the totality of life, as human and spiritual, thinking has its necessary and meaningful function. It can never replace religion, in which the totality of the personal attitude towards God is expressed. But it can raise the "immediacy" of a spontaneous unreflexive religious attitude through rational "mediation" to the level of a reflexively secure, deepened, and enriched religion. In this way, philosophy finally is "sublated" into religion, insofar as it has led man to a new, immediately personal relation to the divine Thou.

(4) The relation between philosophy and religion, as explained above, uses some of Hegel's terminology but assumes a stand opposed to his. For Hegel, religion is "sublated" into philosophy, whereas we claim that philosophy is sublated into religion. For Hegel, in the process of the unfolding of consciousness, religion is the last stage before man reaches "absolute knowledge." It shares with philosophy the absolute content, but

194

it does not yet grasp this content in the absolute form of knowledge, but in the imperfect form of representation. Hence it has to be sublated into the absolute knowledge of philosophy in which both form and content are absolute.

Against this position we say that knowledge, even absolute knowledge, if possible at all in Hegel's sense, is not more but less than religion. In his intellectualism Hegel considers only the theoretical element of knowledge and ignores the total human reaction before the Absolute. Hence religion, as such a total reaction, is not assumed into philosophy, but rather philosophy, when having reached its term, constitutes a partial element of the higher, more comprehensive religious attitude and is thus sublated into the latter. The "immediacy" of religious experience is thus raised through philosophical thinking to a "mediated immediacy" into which, insofar as it is mediated, philosophy positively enters, but in which, insofar as a new immediacy of religious experience is reached, philosophy itself is ultimately sublated.

The Question to God

(1) We have started from the question as from a self-justifying starting point. Inquiring means inquiring about being as such. In the very act of inquiring, our question has received, from the knowledge co-posited in it, a certain number of answers: about finite beings, their essence and activity; about the finite spirit, whose activity reaches being itself; about the material world in which the inquirer lives; about personal relations, which he needs for his own self-development. But since we inquire in the horizon of being as a whole, about all that which is, our question cannot receive a last, fully satisfying answer from finite beings, but only from infinite being itself. This answer is God, and it involves more than a rational knowledge of him, it supposes a total religious experience.

(2) But God remains a *mystery*. We reach him only by starting from finite beings, only in finite concepts, never in adequate, always only in analogous knowledge which, beyond all the finite, reaches out for the infinite. Even when known by us, God remains unknown. Even when we know him, we do not understand him. And thus the question stays with us. But from a question about God it turns into a question *to* God. We inquire whether he might not come down to meet us, whether he himself might not by himself answer our questions and reveal himself to us in a way which goes beyond all our human knowledge.

(3) But is such revelation possible? God is infinite and our knowledge remains finite even when, through analogy, it transcends all the finite. God possesses an infinite wealth of being and perfection, which our knowledge can never grasp. But this richness might be revealed to us, if God were willing to communicate with us. God is a *free personal God*. Hence he may speak to us and our question to him might receive an answer, through God's own revelation. But man cannot bring this revelation about, he is not entitled to it. If it comes at all, it will come from God's own sovereign freedom and goodness.

(4) But we must take into account the possibility of such a revelation. Since we are essentially related to God and since only in God can we find the fulfillment of his infinite striving and yearning, we must stand ready and listen to a possible word from the Absolute. If God speaks to us and reveals himself to us, he will do so in a way which we may understand. Hence if God is freely to reveal himself, he will have to do it in the world, in history. And we, being aware of such a possibility, should stand open and be ready for it, for a possible word of God to man in the world and in history.

METAPHYSICS AS HORIZON*

A CRITIQUE BY BERNARD J. F. LONERGAN

* First published, *Gregorianum* 44 (1963), pp. 307–18; reprinted, *The Current* 5 (1964), pp. 6–23; the foreign-language quotations have been transferred to the footnotes (adding notes 2 to 15) and translations have been inserted into the text. The references are to the first German edition.

FR. Coreth, ordinary professor of metaphysics at the University of Innsbruck, has given us not only a text by a professor but also a work by a philosopher. [1] The professorial hand is evident in the abundant *Zusätze* that in finer print recall historical antecedents and the contemporary setting. The philosophic mind is revealed in the sweep and subtlety of an argument that develops a unified understanding of being through a study of the being of man, the being of things, and the being of God.

The great merit of the work, in negative terms, is its clean break from the Wolffian tradition. By being is meant, not what can be, but what is. By general metaphysics is understood, not a study of some prior realm of possibilities, but an understanding of actual existents. There is analogy not only of being but also of the transcendentals, and as the being of the subject grounds the account of the being of things, so the self-realization of the subject in inquiring, knowing, and willing grounds the account of the unity, ontic truth, and ontic goodness of things. If there is no omission either of the analysis of the finite existent or of the categories of material being, still the fact that the first analogate in our analogous knowledge of being is human existence, inevitably is reflected in an account of personal being, of morality, community, historicity, and religion. In brief, the transition from being as what can be to being as what is, has been carried through in its full implications. When being is the existent, when our knowledge of being is analogous, the object of the science of being has to be the set of existents, and the unity of the science can be only analogical.

Still, however familiar are these premises, and indeed however

[1] Emerich Coreth, *Metaphysik. Eine methodisch-systematische Grundlegung.* Innsbruck-Vienna-Munich, 1961.

classical is Fr. Coreth's doctrine, the result is a new look. For Fr. Coreth is not merely breaking from the Wolffian tradition but also implementing the insights of Fr. Joseph Maréchal. In this, of course, Fr. Coreth reserves the right to go his own way. As he points out (p. 12), what has come from Fr. Maréchal is not a school but a movement, not a set of ready-made opinions repeated in unison by members of a uniform group, but a basic line of thought that already has developed in various manners and still continues to do so.

The substance of Fr. Coreth's development can best be approached through a consideration of his method. This he deduces from the assumption that metaphysics is the *Gesamt- und Grundwissenschaft* (total and basic science): it is total, for being includes everything; it is basic, for it accepts no presuppositions that it itself does not justify. Its method, accordingly, will have to be a mediation of immediate knowledge (pp. 68 f., 233). Though a subordinate use of synthetic-inductive and analytic-deductive procedures is granted (pp. 88 ff.), still such mediate knowledge cannot meet the main issues, for it has presuppositions (pp. 61 ff.). On the other hand, immediate knowledge in its immediacy will not do, for simply to assert the evidence of one's fundamental metaphysical views only provokes the answer, *quod gratis asseritur, gratis negatur* (p. 67). It remains that the main method in metaphysics is a mediation of the immediate. There exists a latent metaphysics, present and operative in all our knowing; it is the metaphysical *Ureinsicht* (primitive insight) in its immediacy; but it has to be thematized and made explicit, to be brought out into the open in accurately defined concepts and certain judgments (pp. 68 f.). The main task of the metaphysician is not to reveal or prove what is new and unknown; it is to give scientific expression to what already is implicitly acknowledged without being explicitly recognized (p. 93).

The proper tool in this mediation of the immediate is the

200

rejection of the counterposition. Explicit judgments can contradict the latent metaphysics that they presuppose; but one has only to bring this contradiction to light, for the explicit judgment to be evident nonsense, and for its opposite to be established (p. 68). Such a procedure Fr. Coreth names transcendental method: its basis lies, not in the content of the judgment, but in the conditions of its possibility (p. 69); and he does not hesitate to assert that "transcendental method, as we understand it, is not only the fundamental method that is demanded by the nature of metaphysics as basic science; it is also, one might venture to say, the integral method that takes over all other methods which, standing in isolation from one another, are insufficient, takes them over and, while respecting their legitimate concerns, raises them to a higher unity."[2]

Such a tool, clearly, needs a point of application, and this Fr. Coreth finds in the concrete, conscious, active reality of the subject asking a question. To doubt questioning is to involve oneself in a counterposition, and so questioning is beyond the doubter's capacity to doubt coherently. Presuppositionless metaphysics, accordingly, begins from questioning: not from the appearance of it, nor from the concept of it, nor from judgments about it, but from the performance, the *Vollzug* (pp. 77 ff.). Linking such performance with conditions of possibility is the *Auslegung* (explicitation) in a sense carefully differentiated from that of Husserl and Heidegger (pp. 76, 91 ff.).

After the foregoing, merely introductory, discussion of method, the argument proper begins. No doubt, the proper place to begin is at the beginning, but some say one issue and others say another is the proper beginning. So there is a question about the

---

[2] *Op. cit.*, p. 88: "Die transzendentale Methode, wie wir sie verstehen, ist nicht nur die fundamentale Methode, die vom Wesen der Metaphysik als Grundwissenschaft gefordert ist; sie ist auch, wenn wir so sagen dürfen, die integrale Methode, die alle anderen, isoliert genommen unzureichenden Methoden in ihrem berechtigten Anliegen aufnimmt und in eine höhere Einheit aufhebt."

beginning and, indeed, no matter where one starts, one starts from some question. For Fr. Coreth, then, questioning itself is the beginning.

What is the condition of the possibility of questioning? In other words, what is the essence of questioning, what is found in every question to constitute it, not as question about this rather than about that, but simply as questioning? It is claimed that the condition of the possibility of any and all questions is an awareness that goes beyond the already known to an unknown to be known (p. 130).

What is this awareness of? At least, it is of the questionable, for it nothing were questionable, there could be no questions. But, further, the questionable is unrestricted: to propose a limit to questioning is to raise the question of the legitimacy of asking questions beyond the limit; and raising this question is already beyond the limit. In other words, to limit questioning lands one in a counterposition. Finally, as the questionable is unrestricted, so it is somehow one. For the condition of the possibility of questioning is always the same going beyond the already known to an unknown that is to be known; it follows that the questionable, of which questioning is aware, must be as much one as the awareness that constitutes questioning.

Still, what is it that is questionable, unrestricted, one? It is being. Being is the questionable: it is the great unknown, that all our questions are about (quid *sit*? an *sit*?) and never exhaust; it is unrestricted, for apart from being there is nothing; finally, it is one for, despite all other differences, every instance of being is.

But we say "is" and "is not" in such different ways: we say there "is" a moon; but we also say there "is" a logarithm of the square root of minus one. In brief, there is a realm of absolute and unrestricted validity in which things "are" *simpliciter,* and there are other realms in which they "are" indeed but still are merely logical, merely mathematical, merely hypothetical, merely phenomenological, and so on. Which is the realm that is the condition of the possibility of asking questions? Plainly, we ask questions with respect to all realms, but the realm of being that is the condition of questioning is the one that must be presupposed for there to be the others. When one states that a statement is merely logical, one means that really and truly it is merely logical. It follows that one cannot suppose that all statements are merely logical, for then it would be merely logical that they are merely logical, and it would be impossible to say that any really and truly is merely logical. The same holds for the merely hypothetical, the merely phenomenal, and any other restricted or qualified realm. By the same stroke any and every form of idealism is excluded. The possibility of questioning is being, and this being is being in its unqualified sense, *An-sich-Sein* (being-in-itself). "From this it follows that there never is and never can be a closed 'inner area' of transcendental subjectivity, for subjectivity in its very performance is already 'outside' in the realm of being-in-itself in general which transcends subjectivity. Performance is constituted in its nature and its possibility by its horizon, but the horizon in which subjectivity realizes itself is always the horizon of being-in-itself in general."[3]

Now we might continue to follow Fr. Coreth's argument. We should learn that questioning not only is about being but is itself being, being in its *Gelichtetheit* (luminousness), being in its openness to being, being that is realizing itself through inquiry to knowing that, through knowing, it may come to loving. This being of the questioning questioner is the latent metaphysics from which explicit metaphysics is derived; and in explicit meta-

[3] *Op. cit.,* p. 193: "Daraus folgt, dass es einen geschlossenen 'Innenraum' der transzendentalen Subjektivität niemals gibt noch geben kann, da die Subjektivität in ihrem Vollzug immer schon 'draussen' ist beim An-sich-Sein überhaupt, das sie selbst übersteigt. Der Vollzug ist in seinem Wesen und seiner Möglichkeit konstituiert durch seinen Horizont; der Horizont aber, in dem die Subjektivität sich vollzieht, ist immer schon der Horizont des An-sich-Seins überhaupt."

physics it is the primary analogate through which other being as being is understood.

However, as we cannot reproduce the book, it will be more profitable to locate it. If the more obvious location would be in the German philosophic tradition, with which Fr. Coreth has the familiarity of one born on the spot, it will be more helpful, I think, to turn to the contemporary scholastic milieu, to which Fr. Coreth also belongs. Accordingly, I shall select for purposes of contrast Prof. Gilson's *Réalisme thomiste et critique de la connaissance* (Paris 1939). It is true, of course, that that book is not the whole of Prof. Gilson, and that Prof. Gilson is not the only opponent of Fr. Maréchal. It remains that Prof. Gilson's book is still influential (*Theological Studies* 22 [1961], p. 561) and that our purpose is not a survey of contemporary scholasticism but an introduction to Fr. Coreth's thought. Our question is, then: In what manner do Kant, Prof. Gilson, and Fr. Coreth differ?

First, then, it is to be noted that the operative moment in Fr. Coreth's use of transcendental method cannot occur in a Kantian context. For that operative moment lies in a contradiction not between content and content but between content and performance; but a Kantian context is a context of contents that does not envisage performances. Thus, there is no explicit contradiction in the content of the statement, We are under an illusion when we claim to know what really is. On the other hand, there is an explicit contradiction in the reflective statement: I am stating what really and truly is so when I state that we are under an illusion whenever we claim to know what really and truly is so. However, the content of the explicitly contradictory statement adds to the content of the first what is found implicitly in the first, not as content, but as performance. Now to bring to light such contradictions is the operative moment in Fr. Coreth's use of transcendental method. But such an operative moment cannot occur in a Kantian context for, while

Kant envisages an *Ich denke* (I think) as a formal condition of the possibility of objective contents being thought, still he cannot find room for a concrete reality intelligently asking and rationally answering questions. In brief, phenomena appear, but they do not perform; and transcendental conditions of possibility within a transcendental logic do not transcend transcendental logic.

If the point has been explained, it will be well to apply it. Kant, then, acknowledges the need of the concept of noumenon as a *Grenzbegriff* (limiting concept): such a concept is of no use to him in knowledge of things, for he knows no noumena; but the same concept is essential to him, if he is to state the limitations of our *Anschauung* (intuition), if he is to state that we perceive not noumena but phenomena (*Kritik der reinen Vernunft* [= K.R.V.] B 310 f.). Now Fr. Coreth would not claim that this passage in the *Kritik* is contradictory, for a passage is just a sequence of contents. He would claim that it is contradictory when the performer is added. For what the performer wants to assert is that really and truly our *Anschauung* is not of what really and truly is and, none the less, that we cannot know what really and truly is. This contradiction lies, not in the content uttered by the mind, but in the mind that utters the content, and not in a formal entity that merely thinks thoughts, but in a concrete intelligence that by its performance means and by its uttered contents denies that we know what really and truly is so.

Secondly, if now we turn to a comparison of Prof. Gilson's position with Kant's, the differences appear massive. Kant is a critical idealist; Prof. Gilson is neither critical nor an idealist. But so radical an opposition does not preclude all similarity, for Prof. Gilson's door to his real world is perception, and Kant's door to his world of appearances is *Anschauung*.

For Kant, the judgment that seven and five are twelve is synthetic and *a priori*. Still it is only *a posteriori*, by an empirical *Anschauung*, that Kant knows five books in one pile on his desk, seven in another, and so necessarily twelve in all. Moreover, this function of *Anschauung* is universal. *Anschauung* is the one means by which our cognitional operations are related immediately to objects (*K.R.V.*, A 19, B 33). Judgment is only a mediate knowledge of objects, a representation of a representation (*K.R.V.*, A 68, B 93). Reason is never related right up to objects but only to understanding and, through understanding, to the empirical use of reason itself (*K.R.V.*, A 643, B 671).

Of the pivotal importance of empirical *Anschauung* in his system, Kant was fully aware. It was his refutation of Pure Reason, for concepts and, along with them, principles can refer to objects and so can possess objective validity only through *Anschauung*. Of themselves, no matter how *a priori* they may be, they are the mere play of imagination and understanding (*K.R.V.*, B 301). But what condemns Pure Reason, by the same stroke condemns realism. For the only *Anschauung* we enjoy is sensitive; sense does not know noumena; and so our concepts and principles have no reference to noumena. Human cognitional activity is confined to phenomena.

Prof. Gilson is equally convinced that perception is the one manner in which cognitional activity attains objectivity. He differs from Kant, not on the question of principle, but on the question of fact. He maintains an immediate realism and, as he very acutely remarks in his *Réalisme thomiste*, "Kant himself maintains an immediate realism with regard to the existence of a Kantian external world."[4] Accordingly, there are two questions. What is Prof. Gilson's fact? Does this mean that the whole issue turns upon a fact?

Prof. Gilson's fact is not the exact opposite of Kant's. Kant asserts that sense does not apprehend noumena, and Prof. Gil-

---

[4] *Op. cit.*, p. 176: "Kant lui-même . . . soutient un réalisme immédiat de l'existence d'un monde extérieur kantien."

son is far from asserting that sense does apprehend noumena. His assertion is that over and above sensitive perceptions and intellectual abstractions there exists an intellectual vision of the concept of being in any sensible datum. Moreover, he adds, it is the concept of being, seen in this manner, that is predicated in perceptual judgments of existence. Thus, "the apprehension of being by intellect consists in a direct *vision* in any sensible datum whatever of the concept of being."[5] Again, "When the concept of being is abstracted from a concrete existent perceived by the senses, the judgment predicating being of this existent attributes being to it . . . as 'seen' in the sensible datum from which the concept of being was abstracted."[6] So much for the matter of fact.

But how does it come about that Prof. Gilson differs from Kant on a question of fact and not, as Fr. Coreth, on a question of principle? The reason is very simple. Prof. Gilson does not advert to Fr. Coreth's principle and, indeed, could not admit it without changing his own principles.

For Prof. Gilson idealism does not necessarily involve a contradiction. He denies flatly that he ever held critical idealism to be contradictory (p. 160, note). He asserts that, once Berkeley's starting-point is admitted one cannot find a contradiction from one end of his work to another (p. 195). He maintains that, if one starts from critical premises, then one may conclude to existence, but the concluded existence will be merely a postulate or merely a predicate (p. 183).

Now, if idealism is possible, there exists the problem of the bridge. Abstract concepts of *l'être en général* and of existence

[5] *Op. cit.,* p. 215: ". . . l'appréhension de l'être par l'intellect consiste a *voir* [his italics] directement le concept d'être dans n'importe quelle donnée sensible."
[6] *Op. cit.,* pp. 225 f.: ". . . Lorsque le concept d'être est au contraire abstrait d'un existant concret perçu par le sens, le jugement qui prédique l'être de cet existant le lui attribue . . . comme 'vu' [his quotation marks] dans le sensible donné dont il l'abstrait."

are one thing. Concrete, actual, extramental existence is another. To think the former is one thing. To know the latter is another. There has to be some ground, some principle, some evidence, if idealism is to be rejected, if it is to be claimed that we not merely think about immanent objects but also know extramental realities (cf. p. 185).

Further, the needed ground, principle, evidence cannot be reached by a deduction. If the premises are understood in a realist sense, then realism is not proved but presupposed. If the premises are understood in a nonrealist sense, then the conclusion has to be understood in the same sense, and so realism is not concluded. Realism must be immediate truth.

Moreover, this immediate truth cannot be anything proper to intellect, any innate knowledge, any *a priori.* When Prof. Gilson adduces the axiom, *nihil in intellectu nisi prius fuerit in sensu,* (there is nothing in the intellect unless it was previously in the senses), he claims that it is to be taken with absolute universality and that it is to be applied with full rigor. No exception is to be admitted, not even for being and the principle of contradiction (p. 200).

It follows that realism is possible if and only if we *perceive* reality. Some ground for it is needed, for idealism is possible. That ground cannot be a deductive conclusion. It cannot be innate or *a priori* knowledge. Therefore it must be *a posteriori.* On this point Prof. Gilson is explicit in a manner calculated to leave no loop-holes. "Thus, no matter what way we may put the question to realism, no matter how profoundly we may inquire of it, How do you know a thing exists?, its answer will always be: By perceiving it."[7]

However, if Prof. Gilson agrees with Kant in holding that objectivity is a matter of perception, if he differs from Kant in

[7] *Op. cit.,* p. 203: "Ainsi, de quelque manière et à quelque profondeur de plan que nous lui posions la question: comment savoir qu'une chose existe? le réalisme répond: en la percevant."

holding that *de facto* we have perceptions of reality, one must not think that he attempts to refute Kant by appealing to a fact that Kant overlooked. Prof. Gilson's realism is dogmatic; the course he advocates is ". . . the blunt reaffirmation of the dogmatic realism whose validity was denied by Kant's critique."[8]

This does not mean that Prof. Gilson has no reasons for being a realist. He was a realist before he began philosophy. His study of philosophy, so far from leading him to abandon realism, has only confirmed his original convictions. For him the history of philosophy moves about an axis, and the axis is sanctioned by a Herodotean law of compensation. This axis is realism, and its sanction is that "When a man refuses to think as a realist where he ought to do so, he condemns himself inevitably to think as a realist where he ought not to do so."[9]

Prof. Gilson's dogmatism, if I understand him, is that the whole is prior to the parts, that realism is a whole, prior to its parts, and so incapable of being assembled by starting from some part and step by step adding on the others. We have already noted the proof that realism cannot be proved deductively. But the opposite procedures of advancing inductively or constructively, if not demonstrably impossible, certainly bristle with difficulties. In any case, Prof. Gilson does not attempt them.

His fact of intellectual perception is not conceived independently of his Thomist system. It is not investigated simply in terms of psychological introspection and analysis. On the contrary, Prof. Gilson does not believe metaphysicians should attempt to do psychology (p. 125). He asserts a general osmosis between sense and understanding, but leaves it to psychologists to work out the details (p. 207). He indicates the area in

---

[8] *Op. cit.*, p. 163: ". . . la réaffirmation brute du réalisme dogmatique dont la valeur a été niée par la critique de Kant."

[9] *Op. cit.*, p. 228: "Lorsqu'un homme refuse de penser en réaliste où il faut, il se condamne inévitablement à penser en réaliste là où il ne faut pas."

which the perceptual judgment of existence is to be found, but he makes no effort to survey, explore, and work out a detailed report (p. 225). Prof. Gilson's fact is not a manifest datum, accessible to anyone, and by its sheer givenness imposed on any and every philosopher. On the contrary, its givenness is vague and its accessibility is restricted. And even were its givenness precise and its accessibility universal, that would not prevent the Kantian from placing the perceived existence in the category not of noumena but of phenomena. "That is why in the last analysis you do not accept any part of realism as long as you do not accept it whole and entire."[10]

Thirdly, to complete our circle of comparisons, we must now turn to Prof. Gilson and Fr. Coreth. Here we are met with massive similarities, and it is the difference that requires clarification. For both are realists: they acknowledge the real existence of minerals, plants, animals, men, and God. Both are immediate realists: though Fr. Coreth mediates this immediacy, still for him no less than for Prof. Gilson realism is immediate truth. In both immediate realisms an *a posteriori* component is recognized: neither attempts to restore the Pure Reason that Kant undertook to refute. Not only are both Thomists, but also both are quite convinced of the priority of metaphysics, over everything in general and over cognitional theory most particularly. Finally, as realism for Prof. Gilson is a whole, as his thinking deals with philosophies as wholes, so too for Fr. Coreth the priority of the whole over the parts is cardinal.

The basic difference is that, while Prof. Gilson's immediate realism cannot be mediated and so is dogmatic, Fr. Coreth's immediate realism not only can be but also is mediated. For Prof. Gilson realism is a whole that one must accept or reject, and with this Fr. Coreth agrees. For Prof. Gilson realism is a whole that cannot be assembled step by step with every step

[10] *Op. cit.*, p. 224: "C'est pourquoi, en fin de compte on ne prend rien du réalisme tant qu'on ne le prend pas tout entier."

guaranteed as alone rational, and with this Fr. Coreth flatly disagrees. His transcendental method is essentially the method for explicitating the whole: for transcendental method ascertains conditions of possibility, and the first and foremost of all conditions of possibility is the whole itself.

Let us attempt to get clear this point about a philosophy as essentially a whole. Aristotle and Aquinas distinguish the expert and the wise man: the expert orders everything within a restricted domain; the wise man orders everything. Further, to call a congress of all experts representing all restricted domains does not secure the presence of a wise man, for none of the experts knows the relations between the restricted domains. Knowledge of the whole, then, is distinct from knowledge of the parts and it is not attained by a mere summation of the parts. The very fact that the expert restricts his domain implies that he also restricts the number of aspects under which he considers the objects within his domain; as the restrictions are removed, further aspects come to light; only when all restrictions are removed, do all aspects come to light; and once all restrictions are removed, there can be no ulterior and higher viewpoint from which new aspects come to light with a consequent revision and reordering of previous acquisition. So the unrestricted viewpoint is ultimate and basic: it is wisdom and its domain is being.

Now it is technically simpler to express the foregoing in terms of "horizon." Literally, a horizon is a maximum field of vision from a determinate standpoint. In a generalized sense, a horizon is specified by two poles, one objective and the other subjective, with each pole conditioning the other. Hence, the objective pole is taken, not materially, but like the formal object *sub ratione sub qua attingitur* (under that aspect which the activity specifically regards); similarly the subjective pole is considered, not materially, but in its relation to the objective pole. Thus, the horizon of Pure Reason is specified when one states that its objective pole is possible being as determined by relations of possibility and necessity obtaining between concepts, and that its subjective pole is logical thinking as determining what can be and what must be. Similarly, in the horizon of critical idealism, the objective pole is the world of experience as appearance, and the subjective pole is the set of *a priori* conditions of the possibility of such a world. Again, in the horizon of the expert, the objective pole is his restricted domain as attained by accepted scientific methods, and the subjective pole is the expert practising those methods; but in the horizon of the wise man, the philosopher of the Aristotelian tradition, the objective pole is an unrestricted domain, and the subjective pole is the philosopher practising transcendental method, namely, the method that determines the ultimate and so basic whole.

Now, to connect the foregoing with a point made earlier, the fact of horizon explains why realism and, generally, a philosophy cannot be proved deductively. The reason is that horizon is prior to the meaning of statements: every statement made by a realist denotes an object in a realist's world; every statement made by an idealist denotes an object in an idealist world; the two sets of objects are disparate; and neither of the two sets of statements can prove the horizon within which each set has its meaning, simply because the statements can have their meaning only by presupposing their proper horizon. Further, what is true of statements is equally true of the statement of problems and of the statement of solutions; problems and solutions are what they are only in virtue of the horizon in which they arise; they cannot be transported intact into a different horizon. So we arrive in general terms and on the level of principle at the type of point that was made in a specific form by Prof. Gilson when he claimed: "I have never maintained that critical idealism is contradictory. What is contradictory is critical realism or, more precisely still, wishing to pose the problem of critical idealism from the viewpoint of Thomist realism. My thesis says no more than that."[11]

However, if Fr. Coreth grants that statements have a meaning only within a horizon, how can he escape the dogmatism that Prof. Gilson believes inevitable? The answer is that he begins, not from a statement, but from a performance, a *Vollzug,* asking questions. It is a performance that begins early in childhood and is continued even by an Aquinas until a higher form of knowledge supervened. No doubt, that performance will be interpreted or overlooked in different manners when assumed within different horizons; but it is given to be interpreted or overlooked whether or not it is assumed. Nor can any doubt be entertained about the fact of the performance. To doubt questioning is to ask whether questions occur. The condition of the possibility of doubting is the occurrence of questioning. Fr. Coreth, then, begins from a clearly known, universally accessible, indubitable occurrence.

Now that occurrence is also the subjective pole in the horizon he is mediating. It determines its correlative objective pole, which like questioning is one and unrestricted. Its name is being; for being is one, since every being *is;* and being is unrestricted, for apart from being there is nothing.

Now the determination of the two poles is the determination of a horizon, and it is easy to see that Fr. Coreth's horizon is total and basic. It is total, for beyond being there is nothing. It is basic, for a total horizon is basic; it cannot be transcended, gone beyond, and so it cannot be revised.

But further for Fr. Coreth being is precisely what St. Thomas meant by being. For as intended in questioning, being is unrestricted. In that premise there is already included the conclu-

---

[11] *Op. cit.,* pp. 160 f., note: "Jamais je n'ai soutenu que l'idéalisme critique est contradictoire; ce qui est contradictoire, c'est le réalisme critique, ou, plus précisément encore, c'est de vouloir poser le problème de l'idéalisme critique dans la perspective du réalisme thomiste. A cela se limite ma thèse . . ."

sion that *esse de se est illimitatum* (being of itself is unlimited), whence it will follow that finite being is a compound of essence and existence and that every *ens* is an *ens* by its relations to *esse*.

From this it would seem to follow that being for Fr. Coreth and being for Prof. Gilson must be exactly the same. For Prof. Gilson also means by being what St. Thomas meant. It remains that this identification is not without its difficulties, for if the objective pole in Fr. Coreth's horizon is the same as the objective pole in Prof. Gilson's, the subjective poles are manifestly different.

Thus, Fr. Coreth would accept the principle, *nihil in intellectu nisi prius fuerit in sensu*. But he would have to distinguish, say, between the way there is nothing in a box and the way there is nothing in a stomach. When there is nothing in a box, a box does not feel empty; when there is nothing in a stomach, the stomach does feel empty. Human intelligence is more like a stomach than like a box. Though it has no answers, and so is empty, still it can ask questions.

Further, for Prof. Gilson being (p. 225) or the concept of being (pp. 215, 226) is "seen" in the data of sense. But for Fr. Coreth being is what is asked about with respect to the data of sense. So far from being seen in data, being, for Fr. Coreth, is what is intended by going beyond the data. For questioning goes beyond an already known to an unknown that is to be known: for Fr. Coreth the already known is the datum, and the unknown to be known is being.

Again, for Prof. Gilson, our knowledge of being is *a posteriori*: abstract concepts of being and existence are had by abstracting from sense; and to reach the concrete there is added to the abstractions his intellectual vision. But, for Fr. Coreth, being is an *a priori*, i.e., the intention of being in questioning bears no resemblance to sensitive or empirical knowledge. What is perceived, is not unknown, not to be known, but already

214

known. But being as intended in questioning is the exact opposite of the object of perception: it is not already known; it is unknown; it is to be known. In other words, the analysis of questioning forces one to conceive human intelligence, not on the analogy of sense, but properly in terms of intelligence itself.

Moreover, we have seen that Fr. Coreth rejects the idealist's acceptance of idealism as contradictory, that Prof. Gilson regards idealism as noncontradictory, that consequently he is left with a problem of a bridge from a concept of *l'être en général* to an *existence concrète, actuelle, extramentale*, and that, inevitably enough, this bridge has to be an intellectual perception of existence. This narrative, it would seem, enables us to pick the exact point at which Prof. Gilson and Fr. Coreth part company. Both agree that idealism is noncontradictory. But where Fr. Coreth maintains that the idealist's acceptance of idealism is contradictory, and so eliminates the problem of the bridge, Prof. Gilson acknowledges a problem of a bridge and so arrives at his need for an intellectual perception of being. Hence being can be *a priori* for Fr. Coreth, because for him the idealist is involved in self-contradiction; but being must be *a posteriori* for Prof. Gilson, because for him idealism is not self-contradictory.

Finally, there remains the question how Fr. Coreth and Prof. Gilson both arrive at the same objective pole, being in the Thomist sense, when their subjective poles are mutually exclusive. The explanation would seem to be that, if Prof. Gilson does not thematize questioning, none the less he asks questions and so intends what is intended in questioning; further, while Prof. Gilson asserts an intellectual perception of existence, still he is careful to integrate this perception within the structure of Thomist cognitional theory, and so is able to shift from a theory of being as something seen in data to a theory of being as something affirmed in perceptual judgments of existence. Hence, inasmuch as Prof. Gilson asks questions and gives

wers, his position coincides with that of Fr. Coreth,
subjective poles are the same so the objective poles
e. On the other hand, if Prof. Gilson were to operate
solely with a concept of being that can be "seen" in
e datum, not only would his subjective pole differ
oreth's but also it would be impossible for him to
reach being in the Thomist sense as his objective pole; for being as object of perception is being in which essence and existence are only notionally distinct.

Fourthly, we have been comparing Kant, Prof. Gilson, and
Fr. Coreth two at a time; there remain a few questions that are
best put with respect to all three at once.

First, then, despite his use of such terms as "transcendental"
and "*a priori*," Fr. Coreth is completely in agreement with Prof.
Gilson's contention that ". . . what is contradictory . . . is
wishing to pose the problem of critical idealism from the viewpoint of Thomist realism."[12] Indeed, Fr. Coreth excludes as
impossible within his horizon not only critical idealism but any
idealism and along with them Prof. Gilson's perceptionism.
For him there can be no problem of the "extramental," of
getting outside the mind, for as soon as a question is asked,
being is intended, being includes everything, and so everything
already is within the mind's intention: ". . . subjectivity in its
very performance is already 'outside' in the realm of being-in-
itself in general."[13]

Secondly, does Fr. Coreth perceive being or does he not? I
think his answer would be that (1) being is not known without
perceptions, (2) being is not known by perceptions alone, and
(3) by the light of intelligence we know whether or not what
we perceive is. In other words, he would not say with Prof.

[12] *Op. cit.*, p. 161: ". . . ce qui est contradictoire, . . . c'est de vouloir
poser le problème de l'idéalisme critique dans la perspective du réalisme
thomiste."
[13] *Op. cit.*, p. 193: ". . . die Subjektivität in ihrem Vollzug immer schon
'draussen' ist beim An-sich-Sein überhaupt . . ."

216

Gilson that we know being by perceiving it; and he would say with St. Thomas: ". . . what those words of Augustine mean is this, that we do not expect to derive truth entirely from the senses. We also need the agent intellect's light; through this we attain to unchanging possession of truth in changing things, and distinguish the things themselves from their mere likenesses."[14]

Thirdly, Fr. Coreth would agree with Prof. Gilson's statement: ". . . the transcendental viewpoint of *a priori* conditions for the object of knowledge is ignorant by definition of the empirical problem of the existence in themselves of the objects known."[15] He would point out, however, that Prof. Gilson is speaking of Kantian thought, and he would indicate the two essential differences between his approach and Kant's. First, his transcendental inquiry is, not into the *a priori* conditions of cognitional objects, but into the *a priori* conditions of questions. Kant wrote an *Erkenntniskritik:* the conditioned is the objective pole, the condition is the subjective pole. Fr. Coreth is writing a metaphysics: his subjective pole, questioning, is the conditioned; and his objective pole, being, is the condition. Hence Fr. Coreth's transcendental inquiry is just the inverse of Kant's. Secondly, Kant's *a priori* is in the essentialist order and so, as we have seen, it is solely through *Anschauung* that it can have any objective reference or any objective validity; further, since this *Anschauung* is not of noumena, there cannot arise within the Kantian approach any question of the *existence en soi* of the objects known in Kant's world as appearance. But what follows from Kant's *a priori,* does not follow from Fr. Coreth's. Fr. Coreth's is being as unrestricted, the whole of all that is; within

[14] *Sum. theol.,* 1 q. 84, a. 6 ad 1m: ". . . per illa verba Augustini datur intelligi quod veritas non sit totaliter a sensibus exspectanda. Requiritur enim lumen intellectus agentis, per quod immutabiliter veritatem in rebus mutabilibus cognoscamus, et discernamus ipsas res a similitudinibus rerum."

[15] *Op. cit.,* p. 177: ". . . le point de vue transcendental des conditions *a priori* de l'objet de connaissance ignore, par définition, le probléme empirique de l'existence en soi des objets connus."

being there is already included *An-sich-Sein*. Not only does *An-sich-Sein* lie within Fr. Coreth's transcendental viewpoint, but also from that very fact it follows that Fr. Coreth's treatment of objectivity differs totally from Kant's and, indeed, from that of any perceptionist. For Kant cognitional operations can be related to objects only through *Anschauung,* so that perception has to be the constitutive principle of objectivity. For Fr. Coreth the constitutive principle of objectivity is the question: questioning immediately intends being; data are referred to being as what questions are about; answers are referred to being as answers to questions. Fr. Coreth's position on objectivity is the inverse of the Kantian position; it also is the inverse of the perceptionist position, which relates our cognitional operations to reality, not through the intention of being in the question, but through sense.

At the end of this attempt to locate Fr. Coreth's position within the scholastic context, I must note that my operation is not altogether in accord with Fr. Coreth's exclusion of an *Erkenntniskritik,* his aim of presuppositionless metaphysics, his projected inclusion within metaphysics of an *Erkenntnismetaphysik.* The fact is, of course, that while I consider Fr. Coreth's metaphysics a sound and brilliant achievement, I should not equate metaphysics with the total and basic horizon, the *Gesamt- und Grundwissenschaft.* Metaphysics, as about being, equates with the objective pole of that horizon; but metaphysics, as science, does not equate with the subjective pole. In my opinion Fr. Coreth's subjective pole is under a measure of abstraction that is quite legitimate when one is mediating the immediacy of latent metaphysics, but is to be removed when one is concerned with the total and basic horizon. In the concrete, the subjective pole is indeed the inquirer, but incarnate, liable to mythic consciousness, in need of a critique that reveals where the counterpositions come from. The incarnate inquirer develops in a development that is social and historical, that stamps the stages of scientific and philosophic progress with dates, that is open to a theology that Karl Rahner has described as an *Aufhebung der Philosophie*. The critique, accordingly, has to issue in a transcendental doctrine of methods with the method of metaphysics just one among many and so considered from a total viewpoint. For latent in the performance of the incarnate inquirer not only is there a metaphysics that reveals the objective pole of the total horizon but also there is the method of performing which, thematized and made explicit, reveals the subjective pole in its full and proper stature. Still, it is difficult to disagree completely with Fr. Coreth, for in my disagreement I am only agreeing with his view that, what has come from Fr. Maréchal is, not a set of fixed opinions, but a movement; indeed, I am only asking for a fuller sweep in the alternations of his dialectic of *Vollzug und Begriff.*

NOTES

Page

23 "to our way of knowing objects . . .": Immanuel Kant, *Critique of Pure Reason*, New York, 1965, B 25.

23 Metaphysics is "pure knowledge of reason from mere concepts": *ibid.*, B 469.

23 "Hence metaphysics is a science . . .": Kant, *Gesammelte Schriften*, Berlin, 1910–1955, XVII, N 3946.

23 "Metaphysics is a logic . . .": *ibid.*, N 4360.

23 Metaphysics "comprises the *a priori* concepts . . .": *ibid.*, IV, N. 472.

28 "oblivion of being": Martin Heidegger, *Holzwege*, Frankfurt, 1950, *passim.*

28 "Man stands in the openness of being": Heidegger, *Platons Lehre von der Wahrheit*, Bern, 1954, 100.

35 "I call every knowledge transcendental . . .": Kant, *Critique of Pure Reason*, B 25.

FOR FURTHER READING

ON THE TRANSCENDENTAL METHOD
IN METAPHYSICS

Clark, M., *Positions and Problems in the Theory of Knowledge*, Oxford, 1966.

Donceel, J., *Natural Theology*, New York, 1962.

Fichte, J. G., *The Science of Knowledge*, trans. A. E. Kroeger, London, 1889.

———, *The Vocation of Man*, Indianapolis, 1956.

Heidegger, M., *Introduction to Metaphysics*, New Haven, 1958.

———, *Kant and the Problem of Metaphysics*, Bloomington, Ind., 1962.

———, "What is Metaphysics," in *Existence and Being*, ed. Werner Brock, Chicago, 1949.

Kant, I., *Critique of Pure Reason*, New York, 1934.

———, *Prolegomena to Any Future Metaphysics*, New York, 1954.

Lonergan, B. J. F., *Insight: A Study of Human Understanding*, New York, 1956.

Maréchal, J., *Le Point de départ de la métaphysique*, 5 vols.

———, *Studies in the Psychology of the Mystics*, Albany, 1964.

Muck, O., *The Transcendental Method*, New York, 1968.

Rahner, K., *Hearers of the Word*, New York, 1968.

———, *Spirit in the World*, New York, 1968.

Richardson, W. J., *Through Phenomenology to Thought*, The Hague, 1963.

Röper, A., *The Anonymous Christian*, New York, 1966.

Rousselot, P., *The Intellectualism of Saint Thomas Aquinas*, New York, n.d.

223

Shine, D. J., *An Interior Metaphysics: The Philosophical Synthesis of Pierre Scheuer,* Weston, Mass., 1966.

Sr. Helen James John, *The Thomist Spectrum,* New York, 1966.

Somerville, J. M., *Total Commitment: Blondel's "L'Action",* Cleveland, 1968.